The Etiquette Guide
for Trailer Folk

The Etiquette Guide for Trailer Folk

MICHAEL R. SMITH

ARPress

ILLUMINATING IDEAS
EMPOWERING VOICES

ARPress
45 Dan Road Suite 5
Canton MA 02021

Hotline: 1(888) 821-0229
Fax: 1(508) 545-7580

Ordering Information:
Quantity sales. Special discounts are available on quantity purchases by corporations, associations, and others. For details, contact the publisher at the address above.

Printed in the United States of America.

ISBN-13:	Softcover	979-8-89356-159-3
	eBook	979-8-89356-160-9

Library of Congress Control Number: 2024914846

Table of Contents

Other works by this author:

- *Razor Wire* (annual poetry anthology), 1991–2003, edited by Shaun Griffin, Community Chest Inc.
- *Lead Poisoning: 25 True Stories from the Wrong End of a Gun* (anthology), edited by Chris Pfouts, 1991, Paladin Press
- *True Tales of American Violence* (anthology—personal stories of surviving violence), edited by Chris Pfouts, 1993, Paladin Press.
- *Brushfire* (anthology—poetry and short stories), 1998–1999, Journal of the University of Nevada.
- *The Illustrated Poetry of Crazy Bear,* Michael R. Smith, 2005, self-published.

This book is dedicated to all my relatives—genetic and otherwise—who have given me the wonderful honor of sharing their lives with me, thus inspiring me to create this interactive guide to elucidate, amuse, and cause people to wonder about life's weirdness.

FOREWORD

You may be wondering as you begin to read this who I am and what qualifies me to write such a unique self-help book. I am a third-generation American from a very typical Okie clan. Some of my ancestors were Comanche, and many of them were Scotch Irish. My people came out of west Texas during the depression and settled near Sacramento, California.

In essence, I was genetically and socially handicapped from birth. We moved when I was seven, and I entered a different school system. I immediately flunked third grade because I couldn't read—which was understandable since I didn't speak *standard* English. Since then, I've discovered that I don't have the enzymes to digest alcohol, so I can't drink— and remain remotely sane—and my social skills have always earned me notations about "does not play well with others!" I've worked very hard throughout my life to overcome those shortcomings.

My relatives have been a wonderful inspiration to me and have, over the course of many years, shown me most of the reasons why I'd like to live in a *tree*, overlooking the Amazon River. Of course, the local Indians would look at me and say, "Damn, will you just look at that guy and his trashy tree house! There goes the neighborhood…"

Being "trailer folk" is more a state of mind or a lifestyle, and it doesn't seem to really matter whether you live in a beat-up, old, single-wide trailer, a big, new condo, or a tiny, mud hut. It's the attitude and appearance that generate the ambiance of "trailer folk."

My intension with this book is to provide a humorous general guide for all those socially challenged folks out there so that they may cope—more successfully—with life's ever-changing situations and not wind up, asking, "What'd I *say*?" as the world seems, once again, to be looking down its collective nose at them.

I like to think of myself as being "recovering trailer folk."

CHAPTER 1

Relatives

You've just heard that your mother-in-law is coming to stay with you—for *three* weeks! Do you

    a. graciously give up your own bedroom,

    b. move your Dale Earnhardt memorial shrine out of the spare room, or

    c. put Mom on the top bunk in the kids' room?

These choices should be considered carefully because each selection is fraught with potential difficulties.

Giving up your own bedroom is a wonderful gesture, but then where are you going to sleep? There are several options. You could displace the kids, put them on the living room floor in sleeping bags ("We're camping!"), leaving you and your wife free to discuss which of you is going to take the top bunk on those twin beds. Another choice might be to sleep out in the truck camper (being extra careful if it's up on jacks rather than on the truck itself!) or camp trailer. Of course, there's always a motel, but what about the kids?

Some people would consider it rude to assume that just because Grandma wants to visit the kids, she's willing to babysit them 24-7 for three weeks. Sending your mother-in-law to the motel is always an option too. Then you'll have to choose an appropriate lodging: Motel 6, Billy Bob's Bed-n- Breakfast, or the Fantasy Inn.

Moving the memorial to old number 3 might just border on sacrilege, by your standards, and could be too *painful* to really consider.

So what do you do?

Maybe you could squeeze a small cot into the memorial room and nicely insist that Mom *please* not disturb any of the sacred items in your holy NASCAR shrine.

On the other hand, listening to your wife's suggestions might turn out to be a useful option—but where would you be if the fellas ever heard about it? Maybe she'd agree to give you all the credit for the idea. Does that mean you'd have to take all the blame if the idea doesn't fly with Mom? You could always try to sell the motel idea by pointing out the great features, such as the hot tubs and vibrating beds at the Fantasy Inn.

Then there's the option of setting up "the guest house" (a tent in the backyard) and running an extension cord out there to power the TV and heater.

Your parents come to visit for a week. You have a couple of brews with your dad, and he quietly asks you, "Hey, Bub, how about a tour of the local topless bars and porno shops?" Do you

    a. suddenly become *profoundly* deaf;
    b. say, "Sure, Pop, let me finish this beer, and we'll roll"; or
    c. take away Dad's beer and chew him out for being a drunken pervert?

Worse yet, he asks you about the "cat houses" in the area. Do you

    a. stare in amazement and just walk away;
    b. ask, "Are you buyin'?"; or
    c. go tell your mom?

There are so many things that could go incredibly wrong in those scenarios. I suppose it all depends on just how close you feel to your dad and what experiences you're willing to share with him. A lot of folks would just hand him a map (with all the hot spots marked in red) and tell him he's on his *own*.

Your parents are divorced (saw *that* one coming, didn't you?). Every time you speak to your dad, he tries to get you to fix him up with a woman. Do you

    a.   follow Nancy's advice and just say no;

    b.   direct the conversation to another topic—"Not today, Dad, I've already had my issue"; or

    c.   point out to him that *no* woman (in her right mind) wants to meet an obnoxious pervert with no money?

Diplomacy skills are a rare commodity among my kind, so—sometimes—you just have to hope for the best. Of course, they *do* say that there's a woman (or two) out there for every man, but that thought just frightens me.

Your mother-in-law comes to stay for two weeks without your father-in- law. She asks a *lot* of questions about where the local truck stop is, which bars the truckers hang out at, and how the motels are. The next night, she gets all dolled up in her hottest honky-tonk dress and war paint and then announces that she's "going out for a cup of coffee."

You don't see her again until noon the next day, and she's not wearing any war paint.

How do you respond?

    a.   Act nonchalant and say, "Hey, Mom! How ya doin'? Want some coffee?"

    b.   Give her a beer and ask her what *she* thinks of the local motels?

    c.   Freak out and call her a hussy?

All the possible choices can lead straight to trouble.

You probably don't want to seem uncaring, but you may not want your mother-in-law hanging on your shoulder (severely hungover), blubbering about how your father-in-law just ain't meeting her "needs" anymore. It could be a bit awkward.

Calling her a hussy, especially when she's hungover, is liable to start more drama than you want to deal with. All that kung fu goes right out the door when you have to defend yourself against a *female* relative. Besides, it's not nice to judge people.

I've never been very good at minding my own business. I'm a "fix-it" kind of guy. I do, however, always try to choose the right tool for the job at hand. I went to college with several marriages and family therapists, so I know them *personally*. I try to recommend certain ones to particular people—like matching up the "airy-fairy" types with the space cadets or the "paranoids" with the UFO watchers.

Hey, some of those therapists really are worth seeing. I keep their phone numbers handy, just in case.

Your grandparents break up during your ("peace, love, microdot") teenage years, and your grandpa gets remarried to someone four years older than you.

During a typical (drunken) Christmas Eve party, your new "grandma" hits on you. Do you

    a.   acknowledge that she looks *pretty* good, especially after three whiskey sours and a few bong hits;
    b.   thank her politely for the offer and decline, explaining that it could get *real* ugly if anyone noticed;
    c.   hand her the bong and see where it leads; or
    d.   hand her the bong and make your escape?

Some situations just boggle the mind! Sometimes, you just have to ask yourself, "What would [insert your favorite role model's name] *do*?" then act accordingly.

While staying at your aunt's house after you got out of the military, your aunt asks you to babysit so she and one of her girlfriends can go out honky- tonking. Sometime after midnight, you get a call from the bartender at your aunt's favorite club, telling you that your aunt is table dancing—topless— and some fool is shooting bullets into the ceiling because of it. He's asking if you could *please* come get her *before* the cops show up.

You assess the immediate situation and decide to drop your little cousin off with another relative before you jump into the weirdness and drama at the bar. Arriving at the honky-tonk, do you

   a. wait for the idiot with the pistol to run out of ammo *then* extract your aunt,
   b. disarm the moron with the firearm and work on extricating your aunt, or
   c. neutralize the armed idiot then figure out what to do about your drunk and *very* combative (not to mention half naked) aunt?

Once you've secured your aunt and carried her out to the car, her friend works on calming her down. She's almost successful. After returning home, you remove your belt (the one you used as a restraint) and free your aunt's arms again.

Five minutes later, you realize that you've made a *serious* tactical error, and you're either going to have to use restraints—again—or knock her out (or both). Do you

   a. opt for something more secure and grab the duct tape;
   b. take her to the local hospital for a sedative;
   c. tape her up, drop her in the bathtub, and go back to bed; or
   d. secure her and go back to bed—*with* her girlfriend?

Moral decisions are always the most difficult. They're even tougher when confronting revered authority figures and role models. As adult children, we do encounter those *really* screwed up situations sometimes and have to deal with them. I'd like to think all this might just help you all handle those awkward moments with some grace and dignity.

In some situations, you just have to "do what you gotta do and go with the flow."

You find your grandpa eating Skippy dog food out of the can (with a spoon). He tells you the stuff is *delicious* and offers you some. Do you

    a. ask if he's got a *clean* spoon,
    b. gracefully decline the generous offer, or
    c. freak out and tell him he's *disgusting*?

Except for the nasty smell, I don't see a whole lot of difference between canned dog food, corned beef hash, or one of those canned meat substances (*intended* for human consumption).

Several years later, you discover a friend who likes to eat dry cat food with Pepsi. Do you treat this information

    a. with the skepticism and revolted look it deserves,
    b. cautiously wonder *what* he's been smoking, or
    c. curiously wonder *how* he got past the *smell* of the stuff—which reminds you of the cat's butt?

Your wife has a herd of sisters. One of them hits on you. Do you

    a. explain to her that while you're *really* flattered, the disability you got for your shrapnel wound from the war is partly because your "little soldier" is *permanently* at ease;
    b. crack open a lite beer and see what she has in mind;
    c. suddenly develop *severe* deafness; or
    d. ask if her *husband* is going to be participating?

Gasoline and matches—that's right up there with the Russian roulette, using an automatic pistol. Once you've jacked a round into the chamber, it's *going* to kill you when you pull the trigger.

One of your cousins is a fat, cigar-smoking jackass. He's *extremely* pompous and full of himself. A few of your other relatives (the *very* few who actually *like* him) don't understand *why* you don't seem to care for him. You

    a. *tell* them very succinctly and honestly,

    b. make a *heroic* effort to be nice, or

    c. explain that you still remember him from when he burned *all* the hair off his butt while lighting farts—and you can't really see where he's changed much *since.*

Your cousin wants to meet you for dinner at an *expensive* restaurant to try to understand why you "don't like" him. You

    a. ask him *which* part of "fat, pompous ass" he failed to understand;

    b. explain that it's really *your* problem since you somehow never managed to develop the necessary people skills to be *polite* around folks who act like *jackasses*; or

    c. ask him how much *money* he's got. Then tell him you're willing to be as "friendly" as he can *afford.* (It's what most of the other relatives have been doing.)

Afterward, you find you're pretty comfortable with the knowledge that your lack of people skills and *complete* disregard for diplomacy has incinerated yet *another* bridge.

Am I the *only* one that's ever considered being laid in the coffin—face*down*—after I'm dead with one of those Mick Jagger "lips" patches sewn on the butt of my pants?

I mentioned the idea to one of my therapist friends, and she told me I was "antisocial." Huh, that's what my *cat* said too.

CHAPTER 2
Urban Concerns

The houses on the block have all been experiencing break-ins (probably by neighborhood kids), and your wife has called the police. When the cop shows up to take the report, your next-door neighbor's wife calls you off to the side and whispers in your ear, "Those kids were in our house, watchin' movies, and took some of our pot! Do ya suppose I should tell that to the *cop*?" How do you respond to this?

    a. Crack open another lite beer and ponder the problem?
    b. Ask what kind of movies they have?
    c. Say, "Aah, probably *not*, bubba-ette."

There's a certain level of trust involved in being confided in like that. Up to that point, I wasn't aware that our neighbors *used* pot. We knew they drank because of the occasional tequila raving we'd heard in the middle of the night.

Our neighbors are really *very* entertaining for me. I guess I'm just easily amused.

When the kids were identified through parental interrogation, the parents came around to all the neighbors and called for a meeting to figure out how the situation should be handled. The parents didn't want their kids to be arrested, so they were willing to hear alternate ideas, such as restitution— while their kids did yard work for all the folks they'd wronged.

We were "the new people" on the block and were virtually unknown. The parents started to panic when my wife told them she worked in the district attorney's office. I told the kids they were lucky they hadn't run across any weapons or explosive ordinance that *killed* them. You never can tell what sort of stuff some people keep in their homes.

The parents *really* freaked out when the boys fessed up to actually having handled a couple of firearms in one house.

Boys will be boys. They made lousy yard slaves.

An eighty- to one-hundred-mile-per-hour wind comes up and blows over most of your fence. Your neighbor has three large, *neurotic* dogs. Do you

- a. prop up the fence and call the fence people;
- b. prop up the fence, call the insurance agent, and spend the money on a party; or
- c. crack open a lite beer and try to make friends with the dogs?

Tough choices.

Remember, in most subdivisions, barbed wire is prohibited—there are safety issues. Likewise, razor wire is completely out of the question (although it is kind of pretty, in a gruesome sort of way).

Generally, the choices are wood (redwood, cedar, etc.), chain link, concrete block, or something unorthodox—like straw-bale construction. Wooden pallets nailed together will also work well but may not be acceptable in your area. You'll have to check the zoning rules or homeowner's association.

Money, time, skill level, and available labor resources are the primary factors to consider here.

This basic formula may be helpful: cost of materials + cost of beer (x number of semiskilled friends willing to work for beer) ÷ time available (don't forget to factor in the weather conditions!) + (at *least*) two additional trips to the hardware store for "extra" parts = total cost of fence replacement.

Oddly enough, some municipalities actually require a *permit* to replace a fence on your own property. If this is the case in your area, be aware that it often costs twice as much if you choose to ignore the zoning laws and get *caught* "playing stupid" (they'll make you buy the permit *and* fine you an equal amount). Sometimes, they'll even make you *tear down* the new fence *before* they issue you a permit to (re)build the fence—insult to injury. Remember, any aggressive retaliatory act will be considered *terrorism* and treated as a *serious* crime.

The truly enlightened individual (or most women) might call places such as Home Depot, where they'll give you quotes on materials, then print out a list of all the stuff needed to do the job. Delivery is extra.

I heard a rumor that they now have crews that'll come out to do the job for you. Of course, that'd be extra too.

A friend once suggested stacking bags of ready-mix cement along the fence line, like cinder blocks, then letting the weather harden the cement. Eventually, the paper from the bags would wear off, leaving what looked like a concrete sandbag fence. I tried to tell my wife about the idea, but she never let me get the whole sentence out before deciding that it was a *stupid* plan. Personally, I think it could be kinda cool... what about for floods?

I lived up in Seattle for a while—twice. With all the rain they get up there, the blackberry bushes grow like crazy! I used to shape them into hedges, eliminating the need for a fence altogether and creating habitat for the critters. Did I mention that I *love* to eat blackberries? The drawback is that if your hedge trimmer breaks down, your yard will *disappear* under a sea of thorny vines.

If you live in the suburbs or in a rural area, you could be visited by large, hairy neighbors volunteering to harvest your berries (and eat your poodle). The black bears aren't much of a problem for humans. In fact, they'll help keep your trash cans clean, but I hear those grizzlies and polar bears are downright *rude*, sometimes.

Your neighbor across the street puts a stuffed coyote out in his front yard. It's standing on all four feet, looking like it's howling at the moon. He moves the critter around the yard a couple of times a day (he's retired). One truck narrowly missed the old guy's mailbox while gawking, but most people actually *stopped* to stare. That thing is a *serious* traffic hazard! After three days, you make a funny comment about his new "dog," and he asks if you'd like to *have* it. You respond,

    a. "Oh, wow! Yeah, that'd look *perfect* next to the sweat lodge!";

    b. "Ya wanna give me a stuffed *what*?";

    c. "Ah, ya know, I'd *really* like to, but I'm not authorized to make command decisions"; or

    d. ask *why* he'd want to give up such a wonderful specimen.

A few days later, you come home to find *your* new dog "Spot" eagerly guarding your front door with a huge dog biscuit dangling out of his mouth.

I still have a photo of the stuffed coyote in the backyard with a male quail standing on the critter's butt, watching for predators as the rest of the quail flock searched for seeds, *around* the cottontail rabbit laying in the shade cast by the coyote's shadow. The coyote didn't seem to be much of a deterrent for the local wildlife.

You have new neighbors (on the *other* side), who have a stereo with excellent *bass* speakers. Although their house is 25 feet from yours, the sound from the speakers vibrates the pictures on your bedroom wall at two thirty in the morning. Do you

    a. dig into your explosive ordinance locker to find the correct shape charge (to blow their house into the street);

    b. put on your jammies to go ask them to *please* turn it down;

    c. call the sheriff's department to let "deputy dawg" handle the problem; or

    d. write them a note, asking them to please be more considerate (assuming they *can* read)?

I've always been a "Hey! Can y'all *shut up?*" kind of guy, but that ain't really prudent in some neighborhoods unless your clothes are made of Kevlar.

Your other neighbors (the pot smokers) have sold their house to a family who has a large dog. He's the territorial sort—"I *must* protect my owner's property!" He barks at everything within fifty feet of the fence. How do you handle this? Do you

    a. make friends with him so he won't bark at you (Did I mention that he has the memory retention of a *dead goat?*),

    b. feed him table scraps with some ginkgo in them to help his memory, or

    c. employ some weird animal psychology to retrain him so he thinks he's a *cat?*

If you have a good solution to that one, let *me* know, eh?

I did learn not to pet the neighbor's lab when I had food residue on my hands. Personally, I didn't think my fingers looked *anything* like chicken wings.

Your neighbor (the retired guy) has an old dog that likes to pee in your front yard. Do you

    a. be grateful that your yard is getting *some* moisture;

    b. use your slingshot every time the old thing waddles over;

    c. hide concrete reinforcing wire in the yard (hooked up to an electric fence charger) for some Pavlovian retraining; or

    d. remodel your front yard so it looks like the wilderness it once was, thus eliminating the lawn altogether?

I've noticed over the years that pet owners (especially in urban settings) tend to get *really* excited whenever they find out someone is "abusing" their beloved animals—even when it's clear that their "furry little family members" are causing problems for all the neighbors around them.

Nature often has a way of balancing things out. Around here, coyotes roam through the neighborhood at night, eating everything they can reach. They consider cats and poodles a *renewable food source*. Leave Fifi out overnight, and you'll need a new poodle tomorrow! The coyotes have gotten so brave that they actually follow people walking with their small dogs, and they snatch them *right off the leash* as soon as your back is turned!

Many people (especially urbanites) are *clueless* about nature. I guess it's hard to understand that the coyotes were there *before* the golf course was. Apparently, poodle tastes just like a rabbit.

I saw a couple of ads for Chihuahua puppies the other day. People were selling them for $400 each. What is that, around $135.00 a *pound?* I wonder if the coyotes can *taste* the difference.

I knew one guy awhile back (a biker), who had troubles with his neighbor's Afghan hound getting into his garbage cans. He solved the problem by serving the dog at a party with potatoes and eggs. I heard he made a coat out of the skin.

I was told that his phone had been turned off so he couldn't call animal control.

You have a neighbor who's a shell-shocked veteran—a real "spun duck." This guy thinks he's Poncho Villa, reincarnated. He enjoys doing "funny" things with firecrackers, such as exploding a couple of them on your bathroom window sill while you're in there taking a crap.

After several such "entertaining" events, do you

    a.   call the fellas in the white coats to come collect him;

    b.   start a counteroffensive, firing pop bottle rockets at him every chance you get; or

  c. decide to get better acquainted and offer him a half rack of lite beer?

About two thirty in the morning, after the lite beer is gone and you've smoked his best hash, you nod off in his living room and discover just how twisted this guy *really* is. In the wee hours of the morning, you suddenly wake up—drunk *and* stoned—to realize that your pants cuffs are on fire. Do you

  a. go into "panic mode," jump up, and run outside;
  b. have a lucid moment—where an old childhood memory kicks in— then *drop* and roll; or
  c. calmly beat out your cuffs while telling this guy he's a *psycho*?

Once outside, you immediately run into a small sprinkler, which puts out the fire. The born-again Poncho Villa look-alike is in the doorway, laughing *hysterically*. Do you

  a. walk away and come back later to torch his *house*,
  b. *run* away then call the guys in the white coats, or
  c. admit that this was one of *the best* "got you" tricks you've ever seen and laugh with him?

This same neighbor (remember now, this is a suburban neighborhood!) enjoys sitting on his roof in a lawn chair, shooting pidgins out of the palm trees in front of his house. He justifies this activity by using a rifle with .22- caliber *shorts*, thinking that the bullets won't hurt anyone if he misses. He also likes to shoot Roman candles at passing vehicles from time to time. Do you

  a. decide he's dangerous after all and call the guys at the cracker factory,
  b. smoke some more of his hash then drag your own lawn chair up onto his roof, or
  c. swap all his bullets for blanks and wait to see if he notices?

You have a neighbor who likes to stand in his living room window naked, watching the world outside. He's old and *wrinkly.* Do you

    a.   call the cops to complain,
    b.   tape black plastic to the lower half of his window,
    c.   plant an evergreen bush in front of his window,
    d.   clean the window for him, or
    e.   wear welding goggles whenever you're in the front yard?

You have a neighbor who likes to stand in her living room window naked, watching the world outside. She's twenty-something and *beautiful.* Do you

    a.   call the cops to complain,
    b.   tape black plastic to the lower two-thirds of her window,
    c.   plant an evergreen bush in front of her window,
    d.   clean the window for her, or
    e.   set lawn chairs out facing her window?

As we baby boomers move through middle age, questions like those become increasingly fuzzy but more polarized. In a few more years, as CRS sets in (*more* strongly) and our eyes get weaker, maybe it won't matter—"I was lookin' at *what?*" or worse, "She was *naked?* Damn! I couldn't tell."

I saw a woman the other day walking one of those Yorkshire terriers. I've always known that critters like them were, in reality, *self-propelled dust mops.* It occurred to me that they might actually be useful as wet mops too. That could be a cool way to help the environment— household cleaning equipment that runs on table scraps and buffalo bones! So I asked my wife if it'd work to dip one of them in the sink and have it run back and forth across the linoleum—maybe wave a dog biscuit around like a magic wand to keep the critter going. She figured it'd never work because the little fuzz ball would spend the first five minutes rolling around on the carpet and wind up *too dry* to be any good on the kitchen floor.

I'm still trying to find someone willing to let me *borrow* one of those little hair balls to experiment with. Weirdly enough, it turns out them yappy little dogs are *expensive*. Who'd a thought, eh? Hey! Maybe I can get a *research* grant.

You notice that your Scottish terrier is dragging a *massive* dust bunny around on one of its legs. You

    a. carefully snip the hair on your little darling's leg to remove the dirt ball;

    b. b. snatch up your critter and run the shop vac over its fur; or

    c. take your little "baby" to the groomer for a shampoo, trim, and pedicure.

Your grannie gives your parents a miniature poodle and tells them, "He's a little *nervous*." You figure, "So he'll get over it eventually."

A year later, this neurotic dust ball is still going *completely* crazy whenever the doorbell rings. One night, you arrive at your people's house after they've gone to bed. You ring the doorbell, hear a lot of excited barking fading back into the house, then hear a lot of cursing, surrounded by more barking coming toward the door. Your dad opens the door, wearing a T-shirt with what looks like a *wet spot* in the middle of his chest. Every time the dog gets near, your dad tries to *step* on it. He's *not* a happy camper. You

    a. apologize for waking him;

    b. ask, "What's with the wet spot?"; or

    c. observe that the two-pound-waste-of-fur is *still* "nervous."

Your dad explains that this fur ball's idea of sentry duty is to yap *wildly* then jump up on your dad's chest and *pee*. You

    a. suddenly understand *why* your dad is trying to stomp on the little hair ball;

b. almost swallow your tongue, trying *really* hard not to laugh; or

c. point out that it actually *is* a successful method of alerting him.

One of your aunts comes to visit and has one of those miniature wiener dogs. As this hyperactive little critter is roaming around your house, *terrorizing* your cat, you see that she gives the dog one of those fabric softener dryer sheets to play with. Two hours later, you notice that your *entire house* smells like the dryer sheet. You

a. figure that this is a *good* thing,
b. start wondering if you can interest the *cat* in a dryer sheet, or
c. call the vet to see if it's *safe* to tie a dryer sheet onto the cat's tail.

Those of you who own dust mop dogs or hyperactive critters may want to try this! Check with your vet to make sure it's *safe*.

CHAPTER 3

Walmart and Other Social Bonding Spots

How about those trips to Walmart? I always tell my wife that I'm going there for "cultural bonding." I can't recall right offhand how I ever managed to reach adulthood before Walmart came along.

My wife and I were at one of the local Walmart stores one day (we have five now!), having the "volume versus value" discussion as we tried to select just the right laundry detergent for our needs. The store was relatively crowded. A tall woman stopped and, out of the blue, decided to share with us that she'd just come from Hawaii to do some shopping because there were no Walmart stores there.

Fifteen people stopped and stared at her. It was like that old TV commercial about the stockbroker where the world comes to a *screeching halt* to hear what the broker said.

I've never been to Hawaii (except for that time on a military transport, where we stopped for fuel, and they wouldn't let us off the plane). Do they have trailers there?

I couldn't figure out why someone would come from Hawaii to a store in Nevada. Wasn't California *closer*? It turned out she was visiting friends in the area and decided to take the opportunity to make a pilgrimage to "Wally World."

The other people there were awestruck and treated her with great reverence.

Walmart is a lot like making a trip around the world without all the inconveniences at the airport. In the rest of the world, you might be mistaken for someone important—like a diplomat or a rich person—and get kidnapped or hurt. At Walmart, *everyone* is important, and they work hard to make it a safe experience! "Hi! Welcome to Walmart!"

One of the most amazing aspects of a Wally World adventure (for me) is being able to watch mothers from all over the world yelling at their children. Apparently, it doesn't matter where you're from. The whole kid/mom interaction is pretty much the same. Kids want to grab this toy or that piece of candy, and the moms say no in a *wonderful* variety of languages. The tone and motions say it all: "No! Put that back! Get yer little butt over here!" It's a free language lesson.

I studied language development as part of my minor at the university. I had to plow through dozens of books on weird stuff, like how children in Papua, New Guinea, learn to speak properly or the subtle and shifting nuances of the Hopi language. There's even been extensive research done on the grammatical structure of the English dialect Black Americans commonly use. How come nobody ever did a study on *Okie English*? I'm wondering if all that money people spent on cultural anthropology couldn't have been put to better use with a bunch of field trips to Wally World? "Higher education" while moseying from the shoe department, past women's wear to the front checkouts.

Have you ever gone into a Walmart and *actually* looked at all the stuff they have in there? It could take *weeks*!

You're in Wally World, looking at notebooks, when a little, old lady asks, "Sir, could you reach me that binder?" while pointing to the one she means—on the *top* shelf. You respond,

    a. "Sure thing!" and stretch *way* up to fetch it for her;
    b. Nope, can't reach it. Yer gonna have to get one of the store guys," and walk away; or
    c. realize you can't reach it and scale the shelf—like an orangutan— to fetch it.

After doing your best monkey imitation, the old lady hands the notebook back to you and say, "No, I think I'd rather have the one that was next to it." Do you

    a. decide this was *just* the notebook *you* were looking for and leave to purchase it;
    b. nimbly climb back up the shelf to replace it and grab the other one;
    c. offer to toss the old lady up there to fetch it herself; or
    d. climb back up there, hoping all that stuff you heard about Karmic brownie points is true?

I suppose the answer to that one depends on how much respect you have for elders and whether or not you can toss an old lady 10 feet in the air. I was raised to respect elders even when they're being a pain in the butt, so I never tried any "elder tossing."

I disrespected one, *once*, and wound up with *boot prints* across my chest. Just because they're *old*, that doesn't mean they ain't *tough*!

Maybe it's just me, but whenever I'm in Wally World, I always feel like there's some unspoken commandment that I should be on my *best behavior*, expected to be courteous to my "brethren" at all times—like acting out would be sacrilege. It seems like others feel the imperative too since most of them are pretty well behaved—except for the kids, and they seem to be universally *ignored*. That's probably a good thing.

There's another store around here (a thrift store), where there's usually kids running amok throughout the store. There are signs all over, saying, "Please control your children," in *three* languages.

I guess them kids don't speak those dialects.

You're in your favorite Walmart, looking for fabric softener when you notice they no longer *have* the kind your wife sent you in there for. Additionally, you suddenly realize that you have to *translate* the labels to figure out what they *do* have. You

    a.   go with the flow and continue reading in *Spanish*,
    b.   study the pictures for clues, or
    c.   ask for a Spanish-speaking store person to help you.

After having translated all the labels, you've ascertained that

    a.   there are *none* of what you're looking for,
    b.   the Spanish-speaking store person has *no* clue what "fragrance- free" means, or
    c.   the product you were looking for has—apparently—been discontinued. It seems that your wife and three other women were the *only* ones in America who bought it.

Having been trained to *not* make command decisions, you return home *without* the fabric softener to await further orders.

Your wife gets a gift certificate for Macy's and wants you to go with her. You

    a.   figure, "Ah, how *bad* can it be?";
    b.   get there and notice that there are three men in the *entire* store— counting *you*; or
    c.   wander around behind your wife for fifteen minutes when it begins to occur to you that you don't see *any* men's stuff.

You look around the store and *still* don't see any men's stuff. Several young women walk by. One of them looks at you and says, "He looks like he's *really* uncomfortable!" (And *you* thought you were doing your best "suave and debonair" look.) When you ask, you're told that there's a completely *separate* Macy's store where all of the men's stuff is—on the far side of the mall.

Ah, well, now *that* certainly makes sense!

CHAPTER 4

Restaurants

Recently, my wife called in a take-out order at the local sushi bar. In the past, our kids have ordered food from there several times for themselves and the family. We thought we'd give it a try. How could we go wrong? The food was always great. It was "the oldest sushi bar in the county" *and* was run by somebody with a Chinese name. (Ain't sushi actually a Japanese food?)

As we were going to fetch our food, my wife said, "The woman who answered the phone is *very* Asian. She didn't speak much English. Be patient." Hey, no problem! They didn't call me "beaucoup dinky dow" for *nothing*!

When I walked into the place, there were three Hispanic sushi chefs behind the bar with two White teenagers—the waiter and hostess. There was a TV up in a corner near the ceiling, playing a sitcom called *Puro* Loco (*Pure Crazy*) on one of the Mexican channels. From behind the bar, the woman in the middle asked me, "Take out?"

I told her, "Yes," and handed her the list of stuff we ordered and told her my name. She nodded and started building sushi. After ten minutes of watching Puro Loco, it dawned on me that I still didn't have our food, so I asked the teenage girl. As she was telling me that it was not ready, I noticed a pile of those styro pacs the restaurants use for "doggy bags" nowadays. Two of them had a phone number on them. It turned out to be mine. I left before the duplicate order was ready.

A month later, my wife and I decided to try "dine-in" sushi. (The food there really *is* good!) As we sat there, scarfing sushi, I realized we were experiencing a true moment of modern-day Americana. The TV was playing some Hollywood "B" movie (with the sound turned down), a married couple was sitting at the bar—speaking Spanish to one of the three Hispanic sushi chefs, four White teenagers were hustling tables, and Steppenwolf was singing "Born to be Wild" over the house stereo. As weird as it sounds, it felt "normal."

You're at a popular fast-food restaurant, ordering lunch, and you have *no* clue what the cashier has just said to you, but you *suspect* it was some sort of a question. You

    a. ask her to repeat the question,
    b. ask her in *Spanish* to repeat the question, or
    c. display your *dazzling* worldliness and just say, "Huh?"

At another fast-food place, you notice that *all* the employees look like *gangbangers*, and their manner is *very* rude. You

    a. decide to leave *before* the shooting starts,
    b. reenact one of your favorite Cheech and Chong skits to see how they'll like you *then*, or
    c. get your food then make a mental note to avoid that place in the future.

So you've ascertained that rude behavior + rude behavior = a taco meal *with* a side order of *kung fu*—over all, an *iffy* way to work off those carbs! It's even worse if they're *armed*.

You go to a fast-food place that serves buffalo burgers. This establishment is well known for its *old-style* burgers and fries. There are framed posters of hot rods on the walls. When you get to the counter to order, an Asian woman (with a *very* strong accent) asks, "What you *wan*?" You

   a. give her your order, take your number, and go sit down;
   b. give her your order and try *hard* not to laugh as she *shouts* the order over her shoulder to the cook in Chinese; or
   c. order the food and *smile* at the *incongruity* of this picture.

Having heard her shout a *bunch* of Cantonese with the word "buffalo" mixed in with it, you assume that there's no Chinese word for "buffalo." This *could* be socially significant information.

A friend introduces you to a very authentic Italian restaurant in a hole-in- the-wall of a local strip mall. The food is excellent, and the desserts are *exquisite*—may be the best you've *ever* eaten. You

   a. enjoy the food while watching people stroll by,
   b. *lose* yourself in the cuisine, or
   c. decide that *this* place is *definitely* worth sharing!

This place is actually your friend's *second* choice. He wants to take you to the Vietnamese restaurant a couple of doors down, but you still tend to have *flashbacks* whenever you hear Vietnamese being spoken. You

   a. figure, "Ah, hell, the Italian place was *screamin'*, so maybe I'll try the Vietnamese joint";
   b. go to the Viet joint wearing *earplugs*; or
   c. take a Valium *then* go to eat Saigon food.

Having survived the mediocre food in the Southeast Asian hole-in-the- wall, you decide to visit a couple of the best known Vietnamese restaurants in town.

In the first, you discover that the food is *excellent*. On a second visit, you find that the headwaiter will *not* allow anyone to take your order. After fifteen minutes, you realize you're being deliberately ignored and leave. On reflection, you theorize that the waiter may have been offended by the camo T-shirt you were wearing. You

    a.   figure, "Screw 'em! The food ain't *that* good";

    b.   choose to be respectful and consider a change of wardrobe before you return; or

    c.   decide to stick with Mexican sushi.

All people have cultural customs, and they often stay with us when we immigrate to another country. We need to be aware that assimilation *doesn't* always follow immigration. Sometimes, we cling to our prejudices and fears. The rest of us need to *choose* how we're gonna respond to that.

In the second place, you find the food is okay—nothing spectacular. As you pay the check, you see a man behind the counter, staring at you. He looks very familiar, but it takes a minute to remember. That face is one of the "target of opportunity" cards you used to carry in the military. You

    a.   make a decision to avoid that restaurant *forever*;

    b.   clearly see that you must have been on one of *his* "shoot-on-sight" cards;

    c.   decide all *that* happened long ago in a *galaxy far, far away*; or

    d.   offer to buy him a beer for the chance to let all that go.

I saw a documentary not long ago about how Vietnam now has five-star hotels to bring in tourism. Several vets I've spoken with have told me that it's very healing to return to Vietnam and experience the tranquility, grace, and natural beauty of the country when no one is trying to kill you.

You spot a sign that says, "Authentic Indian tacos," along the highway. You

    a.   stop to see *which* part of all that is supposed to be *authentic*,

b. wonder why you've *never* seen these things on the rez you're from, or

c. stop to scarf even though you *know* these things are as "authentic" as glass beads from Czechoslovakia.

Every now and then, they actually *are* made by Indians for *tourists*. Either way, they're really good! They're especially good with some "authentic" *green* hot sauce or (even better!) the traditional Wojapi berry sauce.

CHAPTER 5
Bodily Functions—a Social Guide

You and your wife are sitting at the dining room table, playing cards with another couple, when your lovely wife silently rips one off then points at you as your eyes begin to water. Do you

    a. graciously accept the blame as a *true* gentleman;

    b. deny any knowledge of it and say, "I'm sorry, Senator, I have no conscious recollection of that event"; or

    c. point back at your wife while choking and coughing *far* more than necessary?

Unless the other couple is familiar with your wife—and her propensity for flatulence—you're probably going to get blamed anyway. It's a given (in all North American cultures, at least) that the man will automatically be blamed for any mystery gasses of unknown origin.

Here's a classic example of the international nature of this. I was standing next to my wife in the produce section of a local discount supermarket one day when I silently eased one out. (I figured it would help ensure there were no bugs on the broccoli!) Two Hispanic housewives walked by, automatically looking at *me* with a "You *nasty* pendejo" look on their faces. Hey, now it *could have* been my wife, but I was instinctively found guilty because of my gender! I think it's downright discriminating.

I'm all for gender equality, but I ain't sure I want to be around when *that* issue balances out. It could get ugly.

You and your spouse arrive at a friend's graduation party, and you *really* have to pee. You've never been to this house before, and you don't know most of the people. After shaking a couple of nameless hands, you inquire as to the whereabouts of the bathroom then find that it's occupied. Do you

    a.   try to look casual and ask if there's another bathroom,
    b.   go into "recon mode" and do a room-to-room search, or
    c.   quietly go outside and make yellow snow?

There are other options, such as your friend's cat box, peeing out the nearest window or in the potted palm in the upstairs hallway, but some things are just uncouth and shouldn't be done.

You're at another friend's house, where you *do* know where the bathroom is. While utilizing the facility, you realize your shoes are stuck to the floor, and you can't lift them free. Do you

    a.   call for help;
    b.   pee around your shoes, hoping to break the bond of the sticky stuff; or
    c.   toss the hand towel on the floor between your shoes and the door then abandon your shoes?

After you've abandoned your shoes, do you

    a.   go back into the bathroom trap with a *rescue party* to fetch them;
    b.   decide to leave them (Walmart has more shoes); or
    c.   figure, "I'll come back in a week [with a putty knife]. If they're *still* there, I'll free them"?

29

You're visiting yet another friend and encounter a toilet that's *so* nasty it makes you want to hurl. This thing looks like a cross between an overgrown petri dish and an alien life-form. Do you

 a. add to the ambiance by blowing chunks, thus supplying more nutrients for the "science project";

 b. quietly give your friend $50 and suggest a maid service; or

 c. give a subtle hint when you return to the group by announcing that you're going to call in an air strike to drop *napalm* on the bathroom?

While traveling through the mountains, traffic is stopped because of an accident in the snow. After thirty minutes, you're still sitting there, now *desperately* wishing for a place to pee. Do you

 a. pee in a cup like most people do,

 b. relieve yourself alongside your car while pretending to look at the tires like truckers do, or

 c. head for the nearest tree and wave at everyone while you relieve yourself?

Oddly enough, some places actually have laws against peeing in public.

On the other hand, the guy who's in his car, sitting in a puddle because he only had a four-ounce cup and an eight-ounce bladder, is probably *not* going to be too thrilled to see you out there, waving at people.

You're at a department store you're not familiar with and need to ask where the restroom is. The store person is a foreigner and has no clue what you're asking. Do you

 a. switch languages, hoping you have a dialect in common;

 b. speak *really* loud and s-l-o-w;

 c. resort to sign language and gestures; or

d. go into "search mode," checking all the outer walls of the
    store for a sign?

Sadly, some stores don't have signs indicating the whereabouts of
their restrooms. (Some actually *don't have* public restrooms!) I wonder
if they ever find puddles under the clothes racks.

Your wife is menopausal and has hot flashes. As you're driving
down the road, she suddenly becomes "too hot" and rolls the window
down. You

a. *begin* to suspect that there's a causal relationship between
    hot flashes in women and hypothermia in men;
b. start to plan ahead. You put on your coat *before* you get in
    the car and keep a *blanket* on the seat with you; or
c. teach your wife to dress in *easily* removed *layers*.

CHAPTER 6

Camping—Entertainment in the Wild

Recently, we returned from a ceremony in North Dakota, where we tent camped for two weeks. Everyone questioned why I had set up our tent 100 feet away (and upwind!) from all the others. I'd learned from the previous years' experience—being 3 feet from several other tents—clustered together like a beehive—with all the giggling, snoring, and (I *swear* it's true!) the portable TV/VCR one couple had in their tent. Well, that just wasn't what I called a "restful respite." Not wanting to be considered rude or antisocial, I chose to accept the burden, telling them that I usually get up in the middle of the night to pee, and I didn't want to accidentally get their tents wet.

Apparently, that image was clear enough. No one questioned my choice after that.

You're out camping as a group and want to wake someone in another tent. Do you

a. claw the outside of their tent while growling *real* loud;
b. gently slap the outside of their tent while calling their name;
c. slap the outside of their tent while shifting into your falsetto voice and say, "Room service!"; or
d. open their tent and yank on their foot?

One of the really interesting things I've observed over the years is that people have different perspectives about time—different ways they think of it. This is particularly noticeable when people are out camping. One year, a woman I know asked me to build a fire (for a ceremony) then come wake her at "daybreak." This is where it starts to get tricky, and you may want to consider more specific communication.

I'm an old-fashioned guy, and to me, "daybreak" means "when the sun comes over the horizon." At that time of the year in that place, it was about five twenty in the morning. What *she* meant by "daybreak" was 8:30 a.m. with coffee served at her tent. It's weird how we speak the *same* language with the same words and actually said two different things. I've found that this becomes even more noticeable with the more miles that separate the homes of the two speakers. The people from the east coast say it's the time zone difference (and there may be some truth to that), but I can't see where the math adds up correctly.

How about the couple who gets so heavily involved they forget their tent ain't soundproof, waking up the entire camp with their lovemaking? Do you

a. holler at them, "Hey! Get a *room!*";
b. politely pretend you can't hear them; or
c. loudly ask whether it's a *private* party or can everybody participate?

The answer to that one varies widely, depending on whether you're at church camp, a public campground, or somewhere that everyone knows everybody else. You may not want to be *too* annoying to strangers. Tents ain't bulletproof, but with friends or family, it's the sort of thing that *epic* camping stories are made of!

Some Californians I know called me to ask if I could help them gather some lava rocks for a Native ceremony they wanted to do. Those lava rocks are really handy for purification ceremonies, so places like Nevada are popular gathering spots for those (most people aren't surrounded by dead volcanoes like we are). I tried to explain that we'd had some weather, and the stones were under 2 feet of snow. They said, "Oh. Okay!"

A week later, they showed up with an old two-wheel-drive truck. Both of them were wearing low-cut slip-on shoes. The first thing they said was "Wow! You got *snow*!" (Really? I hadn't noticed.) I loaned them some gloves, and we drove as close as we could to where I gather stones, then I used a steel bar to probe for the rocks, marking the snow with an "X" where I found ones close to the surface.

Those guys looked like squirrels digging for acorns! They got their stones *and* a "winter adventure" story to tell around their lodge.

Recently, they told me that those stones have "more spirit" and get hotter than normal lava rocks. They were thinking it's because they were under all that snow. Sure, okay.

You're out camping in the forest with several other people. Around daylight, you hear an awful racket that sounds like a *herd* of buffalo, crashing through the trees and brush, and it's coming down the canyon toward your camp. Do you

    a. *quickly* climb out of your tent naked to see what's going on;
    b. get dressed *then* climb out of the tent; or
    c. lay there, hoping that whatever it is going *around* your tent?

As you're standing there naked, assessing the situation, you see that it's a herd of cattle coming down the canyon, and they're already moving around your camp. Shortly thereafter, you notice that you're the *only* one standing there without clothes on. You

    a. decide you've gotta pee anyway, so you casually move behind a large tree;
    b. move behind a tree and loudly ask everyone, "Don't you people have someplace to *go*?"; or
    c. move your hips to get things swinging then announce, "Hey, looky there! It's almost like a bass lure. I'm *trollin'*!"

I suppose that some images are better left alone.

You're roasting hot dogs and marshmallows over a campfire when someone tosses a couple of *large* "meadow muffins" into the fire. You

    a.   acknowledge that people have been using dung as a fuel for cooking fires for thousands of years and *ignore* the green tint it adds to your marshmallows;

    b.   smack the offending idiot on the forehead with your *flaming*, cow pie-smelling marshmallow; or

    c.   go with the flow and *try* to savor the "odd flavor" it gave your hot dogs.

When you go into town to get some ice, someone smells you, backs away, and *kindly* announces, "Eeuuoh! You smell like *cow pies*!" You

    a.   answer, "It's part of a *survival* course";

    b.   politely respond by sharing the story of the *green* marshmallows; or

    c.   cynically answer, "Thank you for pointing out the obvious so *loudly*. And *you* recognize the smell *because*?"

Your wife discovers that *dry* meadow muffins make *excellent* seat cushions for sitting on rocks and other hard things. Wrap one or two of them in a towel or pillowcase, set them on a boulder, and get *comfy*. When she starts talking about actually *marketing* these things as "organic seat cushions," you

    a.   help her brainstorm for variations on the original idea,

    b.   start thinking about what the people at the *employment* office are going to say when you're looking to hire laborers to harvest *meadow muffins*, or

    c.   smile as you mentally picture half the yuppies in America sitting on a cloth bag full of dried cow pies.

When I started to envision *mattresses* stuffed with prairie pies, my mind began seeing a shift in the *entire* cattle *industry* (with the government *taxing* the new meadow muffin market and listing it as part of the gross national product!). It was too much for me. I had to retreat from the edge of *that* precipice.

A *serious* thunderstorm blows in during the early morning hours. The tent you're sleeping in is trying *real* hard to collapse. When the (*large*) hailstones hit the tent, it flops over on you and stays there, trapping you in your sleeping bag. You

    a. figure the tent's shot, but you're still dry, so it's *okay*;
    b. assume the storm won't last forever and wait it out;
    c. be thankful that you already got up to go pee; or
    d. all of the above.

While you're trapped in your tent, you begin to hear a *loud* roaring sound that you haven't heard since you were a kid. It's a *tornado*. You

    a. go into mystic Indian mode and holler, "Hoka hey!" It's a *good* day to die! Then begin to sing your death song;
    b. scream and cry like a little girl; or
    c. attempt to *cut* your way out of the tent, intending to seek better shelter.

The tornado jumps over your camp then moves off to destroy a trailer house in a village east of you. There's a *reason* those things are called "tornado magnets." Your tent is *definitely* a casualty of the storm. You

    a. make arrangements to have a memorial service for it,
    b. get directions to the closest store (sixty miles away!) where you can buy another one, or
    c. hope you have enough duct tape to fix this puppy.

You find out later that the National Weather Service officially rated this event as a "*moderate* thunderstorm." You

    a. call them up to ask which *moron* was asleep while that storm roared through the area,

b. point out to them that a trailer house was *relocated* by their "moderate storm," or

c. update your vocabulary so that (at least in *that* area) "moderate thunderstorm" means *"seek emergency shelter immediately!"*

You pick up your wife at an airport in another state. The temperature is 101 degrees, with a humidity level of 82 percent. She's flown in from northern Nevada, where the temperature was 99 degrees with a 6 percent humidity level. She walks out of the airport and almost falls on her face. She is not doing well! You

a. return to the terminal then put her *back* on the plane to Nevada,

b. give her plenty of cold water and crank up the air conditioner in your truck, or

c. revise your travel plans to include *lots* of water stops along the way.

Halfway back to the place you're camping, she's still feeling like she is hit by a truck, and she's starting to *itch* on both hands. As you drive, she tells you it's spreading to her arms and chest. You

a. wonder whether you got *all* the poison ivy off you from the day before (It's hard to tell since you're *immune* to it!),

b. make the mistake of wondering *out loud* whether you got all the poison ivy off you, or

c. have another of those *annoying* flashbacks that your life seemed so

d. much *simpler* when you were single.

By the time you get to where you're camping, your wife is dizzy, nauseous, and itches *all* over. The other women at camp *all* give you *the look* and assume you contaminated your wife with poison ivy. You

a. reply, "Hey, I took a bath yesterday *and* changed clothes";

   b. answer, "Hey, *bite* me!"; or
   c. ask the other ladies to watch over her, putting cold towels on her while you put up the *new* tent.

After having a moment to think while setting up the tent, you realize your wife is suffering from *heatstroke*. You take a minute to share this tidbit with the women and *insist* that your wife sit down, stay under the cool towels, and allow herself to acclimate.

You've just dug a *deep* hole (eight inches wider than your shoulders and even with the top of your head) that will be an important part of an upcoming ceremony. You're happy to be able to help in any way you can but would have *preferred* to have had some help. You started off with help, but they went away *early on*. You're pretty sure that everyone else *forgot* you were still digging.

The hole's *done*, and so are *you*. You're exhausted, dehydrated, overheated, and getting muscle spasms *all over*. You

   a. climb out of the hole and *stagger* up to the cook shack for water,
   b. sit on the edge of the hole for a while to gather the *strength* to stagger after water, or
   c. gather up all the tools then walk *confidently* up to the kitchen.

Everyone *moves* as you sit down at the table, then you realize you look like a walking *dirt clod*. The cooks tell you that you missed lunch because they thought you'd left camp. They bring food, water, and a bowl of ice cubes to hold—to help bring your body temperature down. After inhaling the food and water, you hug the ice bowl. After a while, you realize

   a. your temperature has gone down (finally!), and you've stopped sweating;
   b. you *really* need a bath!
   c. your muscles have seized up, and you can't *move*; or

    d.   all of the above.

After a makeshift shower, you feel like you *might* live, but your clothes will probably *never* be the same again.

You're camping in the Great Smoky Mountains National Park. You've been partying around the campgrounds and come back to your camp *really* buzzed. For some odd reason, which you'll probably never remember, you decide to pass out on *top* of the picnic table. The fact that you're surrounded by black bears seems to have eluded you at the moment.

You're *rudely* awakened by having your chest *crushed*, as something wet and nasty smelling is being dragged across your face. You attempt to assess the situation while trying to suck in some air. After a moment's observation, you find that there's a full-grown black bear standing on your chest, licking your face. You

    a.   give *thanks* that it forced all the air out of your lungs, so you couldn't frighten it by screaming like a girl;
    b.   pee your pants, hoping to *drown* it; or
    c.   go for the Daniel Boone effect, grab it by the ears, and give it your *best* French kiss.

After the critter decides you're not a picnic lunch and waddles off, your people come out of the truck camper they were watching from to see if you're still alive. They tell you about the .44 magnum they had pointed at the bear's right ear just in case. You

    a.   thank them for *not* killing you with bone fragments of the bear's skull,
    b.   ask them *why* they didn't do the "frying pan and spoon" thing the park rangers told everyone about, or
    c.   tell them it wasn't a problem. You had *everything* under control.

While exploring the state park you're camping in, you (can't help *but*) notice a lovely young lady sitting in a tree, sipping from a bota bag, and shouting some of *the* most vulgar versions of nursery rhymes you've *ever* heard. You suspect the girl *may* be drunk. You

    a.   pause to listen for a bit, *marveling* at the interesting way the rhymes were rewritten;

    b.   ask if she'll *share* her wine; or

    c.   *desperately* try to memorize the verses.

As you're wandering around the park—together—sipping wine and chatting, this girl pauses now and then to randomly yell things like, "Save yer Confederate money, boys! The South will *rise* again!" You

    a.   point out that the socio-political system espoused by the Confederacy wasn't all *that* successful, even at its peak;

    b.   think back to the *large*, strongbox you found a couple of years before (in *Denver!*), containing over $300,000 of Confederate money; or

    c.   try to wrack your memory while staring at her butt to remember *how* Indians were treated in the South.

During the next week, you learn *more* about life in the South than you will in *all* the college history classes you'd take later while developing some fuzzy but *very* romantic memories about warm summer rains, red clay, skinny dipping, and dancing to a live band singing a *cool* new song named "Gloria" (which they later recorded).

In yet another national park, this one full of giant redwood trees, you're awakened by something furry brushing across your face. You

    a.   have a flashback of "*the black bear incident*" and freak *all the way* out,

    b.   quietly look around until you figure out what's going on, or

    c.   jump up and start shooting *wildly* in all directions.

A really *large* raccoon has discovered the bag of peanuts under your girlfriend's pillow and is taking one peanut at a time over to the water faucet then eating the nut with water. The critter repeats this *very* carefully, removing another peanut from under your lady's head. You

    a.   wait until the raccoon is at the water spigot then holler to scare it away;

    b.   decide to quietly enjoy the scene, knowing that *this* is one of the reasons you don't own a tent; or

    c.   quietly ask the critter if he'd rather have some *beer* with those peanuts.

In another national park, years later, you've cleaned up the campsite, set up your gear, and built the latrine. As you're sitting quietly, preparing some sacred items for a ceremony later in the month, a *herd* of people arrive and start setting up camp one hundred feet away. These people are *loud* and, apparently, already drunk. After fifteen minutes of loud, *obnoxious* music and cussing—the people are *yelling* at each other over the loud music—one of the guys comes into your camp to borrow a shovel. He offers you a beer and asks what you're doing. Suddenly, we have a *community*. You

    a.   loan him a shovel and ask if they'll turn down the "tunes";

    b.   decline the beer and tell him he shouldn't *be* there without a shovel; or

    c.   loan him the shovel, explain what you're doing, and ask if he'd tone things down to a dull *roar*.

While the guys set up camp (with the "music" turned down a few decibels), the women wander downstream (toward your camp) and notice that the stream is dammed where you're camped—forming a *nice* little pond. You hear a lot of mumbling as they return to their camp. Almost instantly, the guys come to inspect the pond. They return to their camp. Shortly thereafter, their spokesman comes to visit you— again. He offers you a beer *and* some weed. He's come to see if you have any trash bags or plastic sheeting you'll sell them. They want to build a dam of their own. Ah, now we have *commerce*.

Your family is going to join you in a day and a half, and you *know* they'll be *thrilled* to see *this* bunch. Joe City-Slicker asks where you got all the firewood and if he can borrow your ax. During the conversation, you find out that these guys are *all* construction electricians. You've seen this type before. They usually resemble an ad for *DuPont* because they regulate their lives with "creative chemistry." You

a. tell him to look around. There's deadwood lying *everywhere*, and he won't need an ax to break it;
b. offer your services as a guide—to teach them *how* to camp; or
c. tell him to return your shovel then strike camp and leave.

After two days of wondering *why* you decided to tolerate the forty-eight- hour party, the stoners pack up their gear and leave. Something tells you to go check their campsite afterward. Once you walk over there, you find that they'd dragged a twenty-five-foot *log* into their firepit and done a lousy job of putting the fire out. Those morons hadn't even cleared away the pine needles around the pit! The fire was smoldering and *spreading beneath* the pine needles and had already traveled 6 feet. This is a forest fire about to happen. You

a. *thoroughly* extinguish the fire then pick up the remaining beer cans and wine bottles,
b. figure you were *supposed* to be here—to save the forest,
c. tell the forest rangers what happened and suggest they check on that spot, or
d. all of the above.

CHAPTER 7
Entertainment in the Workplace

You work for a construction company. It's Christmas Eve (afternoon), and all the fellas on the crew, including the foreman, decide it's time to knock off early and go have a few brews. You don't drink, but it's Christmas, and they insist. The closest tavern is a place none of you has ever been in (actually, that often makes it easier to get the first beer). It's a cowboy joint.

You order a "non-beer" (nonalcoholic beer), as your coworkers begin to slam down tequila shots with beer chasers as fast as they can carry them away from the bar. Within minutes, most of them are hammered and starting to get stupid. As you watch this—seeing your past self in their actions—you reminisce on many of the reasons you chose to become sober.

You've seen this show before: cowboys, rednecks, and an Indian.

Enter the drama—one *very* good-looking young woman, one *large* cowboy (who apparently has some history with this woman), *several* cowboy spectators, one *very* drunk redneck construction worker (who suddenly thinks the woman should be his), and one pool table (with *big* sticks).

As the debacle begins to build, the tavern owner quietly asks if you—as the only sober person among that herd of idiots—could possibly coax your coworkers into leaving *before* the brawl breaks out. Do you

    a. tell her you'll give it your best shot and go scoop up the drunks (by the backs of their belts) like errant children,

    b. tell the owner you're just "day labor" and head for the door, or

    c. assess the odds and choose to make a preemptive move by knocking out the large cowboy yourself?

Difficult choices. You could get hurt no matter what you decided to do. Remember, it is Christmas Eve.

After dragging all the drunken construction workers outside, you're faced with an instant moral dilemma. All those drunks *drove* to that bar, and now they want to drive away from it. Do you

    a. be a crusader and take all their keys then give them all a ride in the back of your truck, hoping that none of them fall out;

    b. close your eyes and hope for the best; or

    c. watch the feisty idiot speed away in his truck (sideways) while you're thinking about the situation, hoping he doesn't kill anyone. Then you choose to follow the boss home (the job *stops* without him) to make sure he doesn't get *another* DUI?

More choices.

One of your coworkers tells you he's a part-time chemist and offers to share some of his "product" with you. Would you

    a. respond, "Ah, no thanks, man. I don't use";

    b. gratefully accept; or

    c. decline then turn him in to the authorities?

Some hard choices. The results can get you killed. For most of us, the decision is clear—one way or the other.

Choosing to report someone is far more complicated and ain't as *safe* as most people think. Even an "anonymous" tip can—sometimes—lead to your name appearing on the search warrant that's served on the suspect.

The company you work for has an interesting incentive program for production. When the workers set new production records, the company throws a keg party in the parking lot for everyone.

While getting polluted on "free" beer, you engage in the manly sport of razing your coworkers. When things deteriorate to the "Let's pee on each other's leg!" stage, you

  a. decide it's time to call it a day and go home;
  b. slam down another brew so you can pee *better*;
  c. feel inspired and wrap trash bags around your legs to keep your pants dry; or
  d. sit on top of your truck and continue drinking, figuring that no one can pee *that* high.

Company parties are absolutely *fraught* with chances for proving how big an idiot you can be. This is, of course, compounded by the fact that no one *ever* forgets the truly stupid things you do.

One place had a "tits-up" award that they gave out *after* the annual summer beer bust. This was awarded to the person who made the *biggest* fool out of him (or her) self due to intoxication.

I suppose it's important for *everyone* to be recognized.

At another company beer bust, someone organizes a wet T-shirt contest. You

  a. ask the foreman, "Hey, bubba, is there gonna be *women*, or were you plannin' to get wet yerself?";
  b. pour beer over your own head and volunteer to be first;
  c. say goodbye and head for home; or

  d. sit on top of your truck so you get a better view.

Of course, if things get ugly, you'll be one of the more obvious *targets*, sitting up there on top of your truck. It just goes to show that there's a potential downside to even the best situations.

You're injured on the job. The company has a drug testing policy, so you have to do a UA before you go see a doctor. You

  a. ask the bookkeeper, "Hey, wanna give me a hand?";
  b. point out that you've injured *both* hands, so *someone* is going to have to help you; or
  c. ask if they can wring some pee out of your jeans because the injury hurt *so much* that you wet your pants when the accident occurred.

Since you *did* injure both hands, the safety people decided that they *know* you don't do drugs and aren't going to worry about the pee test. Do you

  a. *insist* that they test you—just like everyone else,
  b. tell them you'll bring in a sample later, or
  c. start hollering about unfair labor practices until they *do* test you?

After they've tested you, using elbow-length rubber chemical gloves and a pair of channel locks, you decide this experience isn't anywhere *near* as entertaining as you thought it'd be. Maybe you should have stayed quiet and gone along with the program.

You're injured bad enough that your boss and the HR people send you *directly* to the emergency room, telling you the UA guy will meet you there. There are several people in the ER when you arrive. None of them acts like the fella from the drug testing company.

After you've seen the triage nurse, you notice that the waiting room is pretty crowded, and one of the people is a Hispanic guy (with a briefcase), who's looking around anxiously. This is either the UA guy or a *terrorist.* You

    a. keep an eye on him as you watch the three Shoshone women across from you, talking quietly about *you*;

    b. go over to him to see if he's actually looking for you; or

    c. ignore everyone and watch the soaps on TV.

Once Julio asks the nurse if *you are* there, you identify yourself to him, and he tells you that he has to *watch* you pee in the cup. You

    a. agrimly go into the men's room *with* this strange *guy*;

    b. step into the restroom, *fully* aware that *every* eye in the room is on you and Julio; or

    c. quietly explain the situation to the nurse and have her guide you to the restroom in the back, where this test won't be a public event.

When you come out of the public restroom in the ER with Julio *right* behind you, would you

    a. *loudly* say, "Wow, that was *nice*! Thanks!";

    b. say, "Wow, you're *good* at that! We should do this more *often*"; or

    c. tell Julio he's a *professional* pervert?

Looking at the Shoshone women, you shrug and quietly tell them, "Drug test."

While using a bench grinder (yes, you were wearing safety glasses!), you get metal fragments in *both* eyes. You drive yourself to the hospital. After the usual "How could you have prevented this?" speech, the doctor scrapes all the metal out of your eyes and covers them with gauze patches. As he's doing this, he asks, "Do you have someone to drive you home? It's illegal to drive with an eye patch on." You're picturing what it would be like to drive with *both* of them on, as you answer,

   a.   "No, but I'll get a cab and come back after my truck";

   b.   "Oh, sure. No *problem!*"; or

   c.   "Can them seeing eye dogs drive a *stick shift?*"

Having taken one eye patch off—so you could drive yourself home—do you

   a.   put the other patch back on then feel your way into the house;

   b.   holler, "Bye, now! Thanks for the ride!" *really* loud then fumble your way into the house; or

   c.   leave the patch off until you get into the house?

The shock value of a situation like this is just *way too* much temptation for some of us!

"Ah, baby, it wasn't a problem! I used that kung fu technique for extending the senses. You know, the one where ya learn to fight in the *dark*...but I had a little trouble tryin' to locate that curb out there."

It could work—at least for a minute—if you can keep a straight face.

At the doctor's office for a follow-up visit, after some white-hot metal slag burned a hole *through* your eardrum, the ear "specialist" looks in both ears then asks you which ear was burned because it's healed up so well (in five days!) that he can't see the injury anymore. You respond,

   a.   "Well, Doc, the truth is that I'm really an alien life-form with the recuperative powers of a flatworm";

   b.   "Is yer little light *workin'*?"; or

   c.   "Try shinin' yer light in one ear while lookin' in the other one!"

One thing about medical *specialists*, they *hate* those helpful little tips from patients and laypeople. I figure, "What the hell? They put their underwear on just like everybody else does one leg at a time."

It's a simple philosophy, but it *really* helps keep those pedestals a lot shorter!

I did know one university professor who *claimed* to able to *levitate* into his underwear, but I'm a tad skeptical about that one. I'm thinking it may have been delusions of grandeur.

The power at the factory goes out in the middle of the day, and everyone is sent home with pay. The collective decision is to celebrate at the bar.

Two bars later, you and the fellas find yourselves at a topless place. All the dancers are being *really* friendly to you, hanging out at your table between sets. It's obvious that they know you quite well. Your coworkers are mystified by this and *demand* an explanation. You

a. tell them you have *no* conscious recollection of ever having met these ladies before;
b. admit that you work evenings in a couple of places as a bouncer— this being one of them;
c. go for the shock value—smile—and tell them the ladies think you're "safe" because you're *gay*?; or
d. tell the guys you were in there a month ago, and divide up yer *entire* paycheck to these gals.

Be *very* careful on this one! Even as a joke, some things will get you hung with a "jacket" (reputation) that you may not want to be carrying around. Coworkers can be *dangerous* if they think they have reason to disrespect you.

Go with the bouncer story—skip the part about being gay. Don't give people ammunition to shoot you with.

You're busy welding on an assembly line when you suddenly realize you've started to *hallucinate*. At least you *believe* it's a hallucination since you've *never* seen the weld puddle sprout legs and run off before. This is a bit of a mystery because you don't recall having taken anything to account for this! You

49

a. get the lead man's attention and tell him you *need* to go home,

b. get the lead man's attention and tell him *why* you need to go home, or

c. keep working and enjoy the show. You're getting *paid* for this!

The next day (after you've "come down"), you figure out this event was caused by having passed your hat around the locker room, asking for meds to help relieve the muscle spasm in your shoulder. The sad part is that the muscle spasm is *still* there.

Your boss comes into your part of the shop, carrying a three-and-a-half- foot monitor lizard in his arms—like a baby. You

a. smile and say, "Ah man! That's the *ugliest* kid I've *ever* seen!";

b. look really thrilled and say, "Oh, wow! You brought *lunch*!"; or

c. raise one eyebrow and ask, "Was there somethin' you wanted to *tell* me about?"

Every now and then, you find yourself in odd situations.

You go into the office to confer with your boss. His lizard crawls out from under the desk, up to your leg, and starts slowly *humping* you. It's particularly eerie because this thing never *blinks*. It just *stares* at you while it's humping. You

a. try to politely shake it off your leg,

b. freak out and start screaming like a little girl, or

c. pull out your Leatherman and look for the best place to start skinning this thing.

Once you realize the lizard has half-inch long claws and *won't* be shaken off your leg, you

a. rub it between the eyes then pry it loose;

    b. try speaking to it like a horny Chihuahua, "Down, boy! Heel! *Sit!*"; or

    c. start peeling its skin off?

Ain't it funny, how you never seem to have BBQ sauce when you need it?

The superintendent has commanded you to administer welding tests to prospective employees at the water heater assembly plant you work for. You're told to hire five people—unless they're "completely retarded." Most of these people are kids who dropped out of the metal shop to start a *career* building water heaters.

Down at the state employment office, they always tell you to "dress for success." Sometimes, maybe it'd make more sense to say, "Dress like ya still got a couple of *active* brain cells."

So you're having people do simple, flat position, lap joints on steel sheet metal, using an arc welder with 1/8 inch E-6011 rod. This is *not* rocket science!

When you hand the rod to the first guy, this young genius looks at the rod and says, "Ah, 1109 rod. I've used a *lot* of this stuff!" Well, now *that's* certainly reassuring! Do you

    a. ask who he worked for last,

    b. calmly turn the rod over so it reads *correctly*, or

    c. be grateful he showed up with his own welding helmet?

The next two candidates ain't sure which end of the rod to put into the stinger. Do you

    a. show them, then loan them a helmet, and hope for the best;

    b. wonder if maybe *this* qualifies as "completely retarded"; or

    c. figure they're young—hopefully—trainable?

The fourth guy is older but shows up in a three-piece, powder blue, polyester *leisure suit*. Do you

    a. suggest that maybe he'd like to go change into something less *flammable* then come back to take the test,

    b. wonder *how* the hell he knew enough to bring a welding helmet but chose to wear something that's going to turn into a three-piece bonfire the instant he strikes an arc, or

    c. refuse to test him for his *own* safety?

When "disco boy" gets mouthy about being sent home to change, you decide that *this* has *got to* qualify as "completely retarded!" Do you

    a. decide you'd *really* like to watch this show after all and let him test,

    b. to *drag* him to his vehicle, or

    c. get on the PA system and announce there's going to be a "safety demonstration" in the tank assembly area in five minutes—then have him test after *everyone* shows up?

Having a fire watch standing by (with an appropriate fire extinguisher!) is *important* during times like that—even required in some states. Many lawyers would say it was downright *negligent* to *allow* someone to immolate themselves while other "two-legged leaches" (a.k.a. attorneys) would argue that it was disco boy's constitutional *right* to be allowed to torch himself.

There are times when *life* provides better entertainment (for *free*!) than you could possibly recreate for any amount of money. Sometimes, a little autonomy is a *dangerous* thing. Then again, welders *are* just easy to entertain.

Ever wonder what would happen if you put five bikers/welders in a bar with fifty lawyers? I'd tell you, but the liberals would sue me for traumatizing them and causing them to have PTSD.

As you're sitting on the can at work, you feel something on the inside of your thigh. You look down and see that it's a *large*, hairy spider, moving *up* your leg. When you try to brush the spider off your leg, you realize it's *carrying* what may be *hundreds* of baby spiders! You're wearing jeans, coveralls, and welding leathers over heavy boots with tarsal guards. You

    a. break out your cigarette lighter and singe everything you can reach,

    b. pull your buck knife and start an emergency extraction from your clothing, or

    c. splash toilet water all over yourself to drown the critters.

You're standing outside the bathroom, wearing only your boots and wristwatch, breathing heavily as you look at the *shredded, smoldering* remains of your clothing. You become aware that everyone in the shop is staring at you. You

    a. shrug, saying, "I *really* hate spiders!";

    b. shout, "Cheese and *rice*! A guy *oughta* be able to sit on the hopper *without* bein' attacked by four hundred spiders!"; or

    c. ask, "Anyone got extra coveralls?"

While working under a *large* piece of heavy equipment, you become aware that a thunderstorm is blowing in. When you finally decide to roll out from under this thing to check the weather, you see a *funnel cloud* forming above you. You

    a. roll back under the heavy equipment and continue working,

    b. seek emergency shelter *immediately*, or

    c. watch for a while to see where the funnel is going.

You're injured on the job in a way that's going to require surgery and a prolonged recuperation. Because some of this has been kinda creeping up on you for a week or two, you're not completely sure *exactly* when the injury occurred. Since you don't feel like arguing with your boss—

and the workman's comp people—you use your personal insurance to pay for the help you need. Do you

    a. follow the doctor's advice, have the surgery done, and wait the appropriate time before returning to work;

    b. tell the doctor to put some duct tape on the injury and return to work; or

    c. go get doctored by your tribal medicine person then see how you feel?

After the surgery, you've had one *quarter* the recuperation time your doctor recommended when your boss starts talking about how he's going to have to "make other arrangements" if you don't return to work *soon*. You

    a. give your boss a list of people you'd recommend as your replacement,

    b. panic and go back to work *against* your doctor's advice, or

    c. call the nice people at the labor board.

So the stuff you have fixed is reinjured because you go back to work way too soon, and you seriously injure a couple of other body parts in the process. You

    a. tell your boss you need surgery—*again*—and that *this* time, *he's* going to pay the bill;

    b. take your boss to the tribal medicine person to get *him* "fixed";

    c. get the surgeries, then scan an image of your butt, and fax it to your boss; or

    d. send an *endearing* message with the fax of your butt.

The doctor wants to see if your shoulder can be healed without surgery, so he decides to give you a shot of some concoction from several *different* bottles directly into the shoulder joint. You're wondering why the needle is so long, just before he gives you the shot and completely eliminates all your curiosity. He sticks you with the needle and pushes some of the "wonder drug" into your shoulder, then he pushes the needle *further* into the joint (until he hits something solid!) and shoots some more of the miracle goop in. Then you learn *why* the needle is so long. He pushes it *all* the way in and shoots the last of the steroid stuff into your joint.

You're *hyperventilating* and noticing that the doctor's face is sliding in and out of focus.

Then the doctor has the *audacity* to tell you that you look *pale* and should lie down. You

    a.   quietly pass out, landing on the examination table behind you;

    b.   answer, "Huh. Ya *think?*"; or

    c.   answer, "Yeah, no *doubt,*" then lie back on the exam table and watch the room spin.

You hear the doctor tell the nurse to "keep an eye" on you and not let you leave until you're okay. She *immediately* begins a conversation with you as she's walking around the room, doing *something*.

While you feel that this woman *is* quite cute and seems to have a very charming personality, you'd really rather remain quiet at this moment to enjoy the interesting way the room is spinning and wait for your tongue to feel a *bit less* like it belonged to a buffalo.

Preoperative physical therapy is *damn* entertaining. You meet a lot of interesting people, get to be abused regularly, and find out just *how* tore up you really are.

You've had the surgery, and you're back at home. As you sit at the computer, checking your e-mails, your wife *leans* on the shoulder you just had rebuilt. Would you

    a.   quietly pee in your jammies,

    b.   try repeatedly to move out from under her elbow, or

c. smack her on the forehead with the heel of your other hand?

The post-op orders say you're supposed to wear the "immobilizer" at all times. In your *unprofessional* opinion, this thing looks *exactly* like what you always called "a *sling*." The cool-sounding new name probably comes with a *very uncool* new price tag.

You're at physical therapy, and one of the assistants is assigned to stretch out your recently rebuilt shoulder. This person doesn't seem to understand that there are currently *limits* to your range of motion. You

a. suffer quietly, squeeze your eyes shut, hold your breath, and focus on the tear rolling down your cheek;
b. give a little feedback, "Aaargh! That *hurts*!"; or
c. reach out to *the Force*, then watch passively as your other hand is guided to defend your body.

After having tried to ignore the hernia you had—hoping it would just go away—you finally decided to have it fixed because the surgeon told you this is *the largest* hernia he's ever seen. It's now the size of a tennis ball.

You're grateful he's been *so* amicable about your stupid behavior up to that point!

When you get to the surgical center and get settled into your nice (flowered) hospital gown, they give you a shot of "something to take the *edge* off." Shortly afterward, the doctor comes in, explains that there's been an emergency, and there will be a three-hour delay. Would you like to go home and do the surgery another day or wait? The nurse tells you there's cable TV. You

a. figure, "Hey, I've already had the *happy juice*, and there's a *Star Trek* marathon on TV, so I'll stick around!";
b. go home to enjoy the buzz and get the surgery another day; or
c. ask for more "joy juice" after the second *Star Trek* movie.

Once you arrive home, you start to get out of the car and realize this *never* seemed *so* difficult before! You

a. call for reinforcements,
b. cherish the *intense* pain you're experiencing, or
c. tell your wife to bring you a pillow and blanket. You're *not* going *any* further.

You're sitting on the couch the day after your hernia surgery when the family cat jumps into your lap, landing with all 4 feet *exactly* on your surgery site. You

a. quickly but *gently* scoop the cat off your lap while telling it you're hurt, and it *can't* be on you right now;
b. knock the cat into next *month*; or
c. scream and cry while strangling the cat.

You've seen an interesting ad, so you're going to fill out an employment application with a company you're not familiar with. Once you *finally* find the place, you go in and see no one. The front office is *empty*—no people, no desks, *nada*. There's nothing but floor. You

a. go into search mode and start exploring the place,
b. leave your résumé on the floor in the middle of the barren room, or
c. yell, "Hey! Is anybody *home*?"

As you begin searching the *third* cavernous space in the building, you discover a desk with job applications on it. There are also some pencils. There are no instructions, and there's *nothing* else in the entire room. Do you

a. fill out an application then *leave*, hoping the next person ain't an *identity thief*;
b. fill out the application then go in search of someone to *give* it to;

    c. deposit your résumé and depart;
    d. flip over the (*blank*) application then write a note, saying that if this was a test, *they* just flunked it; or
    e. just leave?

After sending in your résumé, you've been called for a job interview. You only have a *vague* idea what this company does. You're very much aware of the professional adage to "dress for success," but since you're a tradesman, this advice is contrary to your personal experience. You

    a. show up dressed in a manner you believe would be appropriate and *safe,*
    b. arrive dressed to go to *work,* or
    c. show up ready to *prove* your skills.

Your boss asks you how you feel about training a kid. You

    a. point out that your résumé *does* say you're a "good teacher";
    b. mention that you *are* a good teacher, but you have the people skills of a crocodile; or
    c. tell him you'd rather *not* train another girl since you're about as PC as Archie Bunker, and you know *damn* well how *fast* all that crap is going south!

A week later, the boss brings out a skinny eighteen-year-old boy and tells you, "He just graduated from one of the local tech high schools. He's all yours."

Outstanding.

He has a good bit of basic knowledge but no experience—a *virgin newbie*! You can work with that. You

    a. begin to assess his skill level by asking a *bunch* of technical questions,
    b. attempt to have a "casual" conversation to see where his head's at, or

c. stick a *tig* stinger in his hand and tell him to show you a one-eighth inch stringer bead.

After you get a shrug and a lopsided smile as a response to most of your technical questions, you tell him, "I'm gonna show ya the *correct* way to do this stuff. Then I'm gonna show ya how I do it, then I'm gonna help ya develop yer *own* bad habits." He gives you the shrug and lopsided smile again.

After a week, you realize you've been blessed. This kid is *exceptionally* sharp!

The boss and your lead man are both the "instant gratification" kind of guys. They *thrive* on being patted on the head at *every* opportunity. The owner of the company apparently doesn't realize that slapping something together then having to *rebuild* it *four times* is a *bad* thing, kinda pricy too.

Whatever happened to doing a job *right* the first time?

CHAPTER 8

Teenagers—Why You Should Let Them Live

Your beautiful, sixteen-year-old daughter is going through her "Gothic" phase and is dating a boy with spiked, *green* hair. After they've spent the day together alone, your daughter lashes out at every male she encounters (which is mostly *you*) with off-the-wall anger. Do you

    a. ignore her;
    b. duct tape her to the wall until she's eighteen; or
    c. be mature and understanding—ignoring her anger while being sympathetic, knowing that she's transferring anger from some situation that is completely unrelated to you?

Of course, there are always more assertive options:

    a. Wait for an opportunity to pull "spiky boy" off to the side for a chat about supergluing his "little punk rocker" to his leg if he doesn't keep it to himself?
    b. Follow Al Bundy's classic example and slam his spiky doo into a door jamb the next time he comes over?

I suppose our responses are (at least) somewhat dependent on how our role models handled similar situations. I think back to some of my role models and have to remind myself, "Oh wait, Ozzie and Harriet never had to deal with daughters who are *profoundly* blonde or hyper-hormonal boyfriends in spiked collars."

I know of one fella who uses a combination of Bundy's techniques, along with creative applications of superglue. He said, "There's nothing quite as satisfying as knowing that there are *only* two ways to separate body parts that have been stuck together with superglue. Use acetone to break the chemical bond of the glue [did I mention that acetone *really* burns sensitive skin?], or use a sharp object [such as a scalpel] to cut the parts loose. Either way, it's really an attention-getter." Amen!

At eighteen, your little darling brings her kung fu instructor home for dinner. Also eighteen, this boy looks like a sumo wrestler. Your daughter has already told you about him being a *very* talented martial artist. Right before dinner, she quietly begs you to be "nice" to him. Do you

a. treat him as an honored guest,
b. give him the third degree like any other new boyfriend, or
c. smile and pleasantly point out to him that "old age and treachery" *will* win out over "youth and vigor" *every* time?

Your daughter is dating a young man—who you actually *like*—and you walk in on them when you come home from work. Do you

a. go into the kitchen and pour some coffee (like you always do), allowing them to regroup in private;
b. say, "Hey, now that's an interesting position!"; or
c. sip your coffee, as you explain to them that some things are better done behind closed doors, not in the parents' living room?

Or the more aggressive option:

a. Freak out, physically tossing the boy out onto the lawn?

A tough call! I reckon it depends on your parenting style and personal belief system. The question is, What message do you *really* want to share about it, and how do you want the kids to feel?

A dramatically negative response on the parent's part could cause permanent emotional scars for the youngsters. Developing independence is critical for teenagers—but so is appropriate respect for others. The parent should

    a.   try to remember what it was like when they were young—a thousand years ago,

    b.   remember that young love causes *severe* retardation,

    c.   attempt to be supportive by developing bouts of temporary blindness/deafness, or

    d.   all of the above.

Difficult decision. There's a really complicated formula for figuring out the "middle ground" on anything statistically, but most of us just go for what we think is *right*. The cool part is that with *two* parents (assuming you are both taking an active part in the adventure), the *great* ideas are almost always balanced automatically by the profoundly stupid ones. No sophisticated math needed!

Your daughter and her boyfriend (the one you like) are moving to another state, and they've asked you to drive the moving truck (while towing her car). Do you

    a.   accept then take complete control of the move;

    b.   point out that they *could* do it without you; or

    c.   feel honored then quietly oversee the preparations, giving encouragement often?

While putting tire chains on the moving truck—in the slush and blinding snow—you're thinking about how it's almost a moot point since the brakes on this piece of crap work so poorly that it's pretty much just a heavy *toboggan* anyway, and the kids call over the walkie-talkie to ask what's taking so long. Do you

    a.   turn off the two-way radio instead of hitting the "send" button and actually saying what's on your mind,

    b.   quietly place the radio *under* the tire chain,

    c.   hand the walkie-talkie to your wife and have *her* answer them, or

    d.   toss the radio in front of the semi rig that's passing *3 feet* behind you?

In a situation like that, some choices are *infinitely* more satisfying than others, but they're almost always more expensive and usually *not* the right choice.

Another of life's little struggles are money versus instant gratification.

After having taken *twelve hours* to get where you'd have been in three hours in *dry* weather, you notice that the restraining straps have come loose, and the car you're towing is almost completely off the dolly it was attached to. You have *no* idea why this vehicle is still with you. This would probably fall into the "miracle" category. You

    a.   decide to have lunch and deal with this problem later;

    b.   freak out, say thirteen Hail Marys, then go do lunch; or

    c.   decide it's time to take up drinking again.

After lunch, you examine the dolly and find the *safety chains* which were frozen into a ball of ice (so you didn't know they were there!) when you rented the equipment. The nice man at the U-Haul place obviously forgot to mention them. You

    a.   add that bit of information to *the* long list of other complaints you plan to share with the rental guys at the destination end of your journey;

    b.   hook everything up correctly now that you know about the "extra" equipment;

    c.   hook everything up, then say thirteen *more* Hail Marys, and hit the road; or

    d.   all the above.

When you arrive at the end of your *winter odyssey*, the rental guy looks at your list of equipment problems and tells you that *most* of the vehicles on his lot are "red tagged" and can't be sent out until they're repaired, but he can't afford to have them fixed. You

    a.   point out that it ain't *your* problem,

    b.   tell him you'll do him a favor and park the truck down at the harbor with the keys *in* it, or

    c.   suggest that he *sell* them "as is" and get some trucks that work.

Your daughter is going to get married and has asked your wife to attend a Bridal Faire to collect brochures from vendors. Naturally, your wife *insists* that you go *with* her. You

    a.   suggest *several* others who would *all* appreciate the opportunity to go,

    b.   shoot yourself in the foot so you don't have to go, or

    c.   put on your best "*stoic* Indian look" and try to keep your mind focused on fishing a trout stream.

When you arrive at the bridal fair, you crack *up* when you see a *large* sign (just outside) that says, "Husband's Corner," with a big-screen TV under it, showing NFL playoffs. Apparently, you're not the *only* one who feels *completely* out of place at this event.

Once inside, you quickly realize that it's simple to figure out which vendors are giving out samples of cake. They're the ones *surrounded* by the *largest* women. As you squeeze by, you

    a.   think to yourself, *Yup*, that's *gonna make yer butt look* too big;

    b.   hope you find a vendor that actually serves *food*; or

    c.   test-drive some of the cake for yourself and suddenly understand why the women won't *leave* those vendors.

CHAPTER 9
The Weed Patch

You've gone to northern California for a class at a tech school and decided to visit some relatives you haven't seen in a while. As you're winding down from the long, harrowing drive, chatting with your cousin, he tells you that although Grannie passed away back in the spring, he's still using the permit she got (for her glaucoma) to grow a couple of marijuana plants. When you step out into the backyard, you're *astounded* to see forty pot plants the size of small trees!

Apparently, Grannie *really* liked those "*special* brownies" and "special spaghetti sauce."

This looks like a forest. These things are seven feet tall, five feet across, and you can smell the buds from ten feet away! Do you

    a.   try to act nonchalant like these pot trees are nothing new for you. "Hey, bud, nice buds?";

    b.   calmly ask, "Just exactly how many plants are ya *supposed* to have?"; or

    c.   suddenly remember that you're supposed to be at the tech school five minutes ago?

Or the more accepting options:

a. Enjoy the lovely smell while your wife offers growing tips for the plants that ain't doing so well. "Old coffee grounds…"
b. Remind yourself that this is an economically depressed area, where every fourth person you see has dreadlocks. Different places, different customs—go with the flow.

The next morning, at the tech school, you're admiring the shapely young woman skinny-dipping in the pond, as your wife is pointing out the sign that says, "No Swimming." You respond,

a. "Hey, do ya suppose she needs help?";
b. "What sign?"; or
c. "Ah, maybe we oughta wander off this way…"

Often times, a delicate balance must be reached between what we see as a potentially entertaining event, and what we *know* will be a source of problems in our personal lives. It's the classic "bird in the pond versus bird with a *big* stick standing next to you" scenario.

When self-preservation *doesn't* override self-indulgence, it becomes a case of natural selection. If you're too stupid to do what's *best* for you, then you're probably *not* going to survive.

As you sit in the classroom, the heat and humidity combine to overwhelm you, leaving you *very* drowsy, struggling to not become completely *comatose*. The instructor is a hyperactive guy who just keeps going on and on and on like that damn *bunny* on the commercial. You

a. wonder what the instructor *took* (smoked?) to be so damn energetic;
b. ask whether you can have some of whatever *he* smoked; or
c. give up, turn on your little tape recorder, and pass out.

While making a trip to the bathroom, you discover the *true* beauty of construction with straw bale and recycled materials. Aside from actually looking kinda nice like a very comfortable cave, the temperature inside is twenty degrees cooler than outside because of the way it's built. You

a. decide you're not leaving the restroom until the rainy season sets in;

b. call your banker (from inside the bathroom) to get a home improvement loan to build a straw bale addition on *your* house; or

c. call your boss, quit your job, and become a bathroom attendant at the hippy school.

When your wife discovers how cool the women's room is, you

a. have to *pay* several women to *drag* her out so you can leave;

b. send her a note, telling her about the home loan for the new improvement; or

c. send her a note suggesting that she become a bathroom attendant *too*.

At lunchtime, one of the staff comes around with a menu from the local deli and takes orders. It *looks* like an average deli sandwich menu, so you figure it's safe. You order "the works."

When your sandwich arrives, you immediately notice that it's *immense*. It comes in its *own* grocery bag. As you remove the wrapper from this culinary masterpiece, you find that there are more different types of *sprouts* in this thing than you even knew *existed*—some roast beast and a *bushel* of other veggies you can't identify. This sandwich weighs 4 pounds! You

a. call the local rancheria to see if there are any kids there who need to be fed;

b. ask *all* the impoverished hippies around you if they'd like to share some of your "*truckload* of sandwich"; or

c. figure—with this heat—leftovers are *completely* out of the question (they'd probably *poison* you!), so you ask where you can find the compost heap.

CHAPTER 10

Life on the Red Road

A Native elder asks you to take him out into the woods to help him gather some materials for making sacred items. As you're walking back toward your truck, you see the forest service law enforcement (tree cop) pull up. Do you

    a. ask the elder, "Do ya suppose we shoulda got a *permit* for this?";

    b. stand tall, assuming it's your Native *right* to gather sacred items on what used to be *your* lands; or

    c. swallow hard, keep moving forward, and hope no one gets shot?

As you arrive at the truck with two pieces of mountain mahogany (5" × 40") in one arm and a chain saw in the other, the tree cop asks, "Do you have a permit for that firewood?" You respond,

    a. "Don't *have* any firewood,"

    b. "This wood is for the stems of the sacred pipes this elder makes,"

    c. "This is a *very* sacred wood. It would be bad juju to *burn* it!" or

    d.   use the Jedi mind trick (*without* the little gesture since your hands are full). "You *don't see* any wood. Go about your business."

So as you're sitting in the tree cop's truck, getting a warning ticket, do you

    a.   stare at the M-16 assault rifle hanging from the inside of his roof, trying to resist the temptation to put fingerprints *all* over it;

    b.   maintain an aggressive and militant attitude about Native rights;

    c.   act friendly, knowing that you're saving the elder from having to deal with this tree cop; or

    d.   figure the Jedi mind trick *ricocheted* off the Tree Cop's shaved head?

Situations like this are the sort that *epic* stories are made from— "The Adventures of Grandpa and the Tree Cops…"—especially after you've both had to meet with the archeologist and head ranger from the forest service to explain what it was you were doing out there in the forest in the first place.

Archeologists are actually very entertaining because they've usually read so much about what someone *else* thought they knew about something. It's kind of weird, having to explain to someone with a PhD that they *really* don't know as much as they believed they did. Do you

    a.   politely listen to what they believe they know then present as much evidence as possible to help educate them;

    b.   get belligerent and say, "Aah, you don't know Jack S…!"; or

    c.   act like a kid in a candy store when the elder breaks out photos *you've* never seen before?

That answer gets back to how socially handicapped a person is going into a situation like this. An Indian and Okie background can quickly zero out a higher education, leaving you completely ill-equipped to handle some situations intelligently. Sometimes, all you can do is smile and hope for the best.

You've been out drinking all night with some Apaches, and you pass out. When you wake up, you realize you're staked out (four-pointed) over an anthill (*big red* ants!). The Apaches are leaning against a pickup truck, watching you. You

    a.   scream like a little girl;
    b.   scream like a little girl and beg for mercy;
    c.   pull out your "bag of cusswords" and start stringing all the four- letter words together, making *complete* sentences; or
    d.   quietly ask the ants to leave you alone.

Indian warriors like to do "heart checks" to see what a person is made of and how they'll respond to stressful situations. If you find yourself in such a situation, try to put your mind into "mystic Indian mode" and represent yourself in an *epic* manner.

You're sitting in a sweat lodge with nineteen other people when the fire department shows up. Once you're certain they're *not* going to go away, you open the door and crawl out to greet them. Half the men in the lodge come out to join you.

So there are seven large, sweaty Indians (in swimming trunks) looking at five firemen in T-shirts and turnout pants. The engine captain asks, "What exactly are you doing here?" You respond,

    a.   "Purification ceremony. It's an Indian thing,"
    b.   "Native spiritual ceremony," or
    c.   "Sweat lodge ceremony. Come on in. We'll roast *anybody*!"

When the captain asks whether you have a permit for the fire, outside the lodge (to heat the lava rocks), you respond,

    a.   "Huh, never *needed* one before you came along";

b. "Is that a *new* thing? My elders didn't mention those when I learned these ways";

c. "Huh. I wonder if them Catholics get permits for those little fires they have in *their* churches?"; or

d. "Nope. *Tried* to call *four times*, but you never answered the phone. *Done* with that now."

Social perspectives. It's all in how you look at it.

Your stuffed coyote, Spot, is in the backyard, leaning against a maple tree, looking like he's howling up into the tree. Everyone is getting ready for a sweat lodge ceremony. One of the women stops you as you walk by to ask, "What's your dog looking at? He's been staring up into that tree for a *long* time." Your favorite elder, Uncle Dave, is sitting next to her, assessing the situation. You

a. stare at her, *astounded* that she's actually *serious*;

b. laugh quietly, as your uncle points out to her, "It's a *coyote*, and it's *stuffed*"; or

c. crack *up* as you realize that she's actually having trouble understanding this.

Your uncle has a *lot* of coyote medicine himself and is having way too much fun with this!

After a sweat lodge ceremony, it's customary for everyone to share food, potluck style. While eating a variety of unknown foods, you encounter something which looks exactly like potato salad but tastes like *mold*. You

a. choke down the mouthful you have and politely avoid the rest;

b. spit it out and holler, "Cheese and rice! That stuff *sucks*!"; or

c. quietly spit it out then go read the label, suspecting it's some sort of "hippy food."

So you've read the label on the potato salad and realized the "mold" taste was *feta cheese*. You

    a. ask the group, "Hey! Who brought that potato salad from the hippy store?";

    b. quietly suggest to *several* people that it just *ain't right* for potato salad to have stuff like feta cheese in it; or

    c. quietly remind yourself to be more vigilant in selecting foods at potlucks.

You're talking with someone from another tribe/ethnic group, and he says, "I don't know much about traditional religious practice, but…" And he proceeds to go on for fifteen minutes, telling you everything he's ever heard about how *his* people do things. This is all information you already knew. Do you

    a. add more information to his collection of hearsay,

    b. nod your head and grunt once in a while, or

    c. offer to introduce him to someone who can enlighten him?

You're at Home Depot, wearing your hair in a single, long braid when a guy whips off his baseball cap to reveal a *lot* of scalps as he asks, "Do you ever *sell* any of your hair?" Your wife just smiles and stares. Do you

    a. rapidly flash through all the old jokes you've heard about bald scalps being lousy lodge decorations;

    b. ask how much money he's *got*;

    c. offer to sell someone *else's* hair; or

    d. just say, "Huh?"

You're in a sweat lodge, doing ceremony with a mixed group—men and women (mostly non-Indians)—when the door opens, and you suddenly realize several of the women are *topless*. Would you

    a. express surprise, "Oh, wow! Where'd *those* come from?";

    b.   politely hint, "Huh, wasn't expecting to *see* any of *those*"; or

    c.   quietly focus on the stones, pointedly *ignoring* the show?

Sometimes, it's not prudent to assume that everyone knows the "rules" for situations they may never have encountered before. A little teaching beforehand is often a *good* thing.

Ignorance is preventable (usually).

We just returned from a sun dance ceremony in North Dakota. I called my dad. He asked (innocently), "How was your rain dance?"

I corrected him, "Sun dance."

"Oh, yeah," he replied. "Sun dance. So how was it?"

I had to laugh. "It *rained*," I told him. "Maybe we were doing the *wrong* steps, eh?"

You're in a night ceremony. All the windows are blacked out. All the mirrors and glass objects are covered. As the alter is being set, everyone is told, "Once we begin, you may hear or see things around you. Those are spirits, but only the *good* ones are allowed in. They will *not* hurt you." Then the lights go out, and the drum starts. You

    a.   respectfully sit with an open mind to see what happens;

    b.   quietly sit, anxiously;

    c.   start singing at the appropriate time; or

    d.   fidget, wishing you'd gone pee *before* the ceremony started.

You hear and *feel large*, feathered wings flapping around the room, then you hear, feel, and *smell* buffalo snorting and moving around you. Do you

    a.   cling *tenaciously* to your "open mind" and wait to see what happens,

    b.   quietly have a panic attack,

    c.   sing *louder*, or

    d.   pray you don't pee your pants?

The buffalo spirit *bumps* you (hard!) and blows *snot* all over your neck and ear. Do you

    a. envision your "open mind" running down your neck with the buffalo snot;
    b. freak *all* the way out and flee, screaming like a little girl;
    c. laugh and sing *really* loud; or
    d. pee your pants?

Screaming like a little girl and fleeing is an option that—while it *would* be *damn* entertaining—might be considered socially unacceptable, perhaps even *rude*. On the rez, it would give people something to talk about for *years*!

Peeing your pants is an option that could work—if you're wearing dark clothes—but could be *very* uncomfortable in subzero temperatures.

The oldest elder you know decides it's time you learned how to locate and dig up *the* best local medicine known to the tribe. You

    a. recognize the honor he has shown you and go forward with great respect,
    b. try to assimilate this knowledge as thoroughly as possible, or
    c. keep driving while asking questions and studying *everything* you see.

Grandpa shows you the plant and explains how to dig it up then turns you loose to handle it. After five minutes, he asks if you've gotten it yet. You answer,

    a. "No. I got *ants*, really *big black* ones, and they *ain't* thrilled with my company!";
    b. "No. I'm tryin' to organize all the little helpers Spirit *sent* me"; or
    c. "Ah, I'm tryin' to apologize to all these critters—then I'll move to another spot."

Once you've dug up three or four of these things, you observe, "Wow! These must have *really* been hard to dig up before we had picks and shovels!"

Grandpa just says, "Uh-huh."

When you decide you've got enough, the elder informs you that you're gathering medicine for the entire *community*. Two hours later, you're covered with dirt and *reek*, so you look *and* smell like the medicine you've gathered.

Two days later, you're getting calls from people you didn't even *know you* knew. It's amazing how friendly people get when you're the *only* one who's got something they want! You

    a.   change your phone number,

    b.   decide to make someone else popular and give *all* the medicine to *them*, or

    c.   follow the elder's advice and give the medicine to all who ask for it.

As you've walked along your spiritual path, you've had many mentors. Some of their teachings are somewhat different than those learned by the people currently around you. Your position on all the different perspectives is "each to his/her own"—but you're also aware that such differences are the sort of issues *wars* are fought over. Whenever you "step in someone else's dogma," you

    a.   show respect as long as they respect *your* beliefs;

    b.   make subtle comments like, "Oh great *pious* one, please feel *free* to bite my butt!";

    c.   smile and nod your head while thinking about how the gene pool *obviously* needs some *chlorine*; or

    d.   point out that you served in the military to protect the rights of others to practice any belief they want—no matter *how stupid* it is.

I suppose the final analysis comes down to what sort of mixture of faith and common sense you're working with. On the surface, "faith" and "common sense" seem like oxymorons, but as I see it, if you are going to be *spiritual*, you've got to have *both*, or things get stupid in a *hurry*.

Never drink Kool-Aid with highly faithful people who *don't* have common sense!

You go out into the forest with a group of people from the sweat lodge to gather firewood. You *do* have a permit. There are seven guys, three chain saws, three pickups, and an "urban-assault vehicle." Naturally, the chain saws are in poor to moderate states of repair, so they're much like the men wielding them—only good for five to seven minutes of work before they shut down for rest.

The chain saw you have was a *gift*. After having read the owner's manual, where the first words you encountered (in *bold* caps) said, "For occasional use only," you really never developed any expectations for this thing. It worked okay *last* year, but now, it acts like you should sign it up for Medicare. You

    a. nurse it along to get the job done *then* take it to the shop for repairs,

    b. run it until it dies and add it to the art deco wind chime you made out of the *last* two chain saws you had, or

    c. gift it to someone *else*.

After rereading the manual and doing the repair work yourself, the "disposable chain saw" is ready to go sort of. It's obvious that this thing is probably *never* going to run the way it did last year (when it was new). You

    a. run it until it stops then toss it over your left shoulder;

    b. put a *real* chain saw on layaway and pay it off with the money you saved on *not* buying your kid a skateboard for Christmas; or

    c. ask Santa for a *real* saw, which was actually designed to be *used*.

So on the next wood gathering trip, you find yourself in the forest with three women, two soccer-mom mobiles (a.k.a. SUVs), one pickup truck, and one *wannabe* chain saw. You

    a. hopefully, fire up the "*alleged* chain saw" and do what you can;

    b. hold the defunct saw under your neck, moving your head back and forth, hoping to *kill* yourself; or

    c. tell the women you haven't got a *clue* what to do and ask *them* for suggestions.

After they've loaded all three vehicles with wood you hadn't even *noticed*—*without* using the saw—you take care of the *really* important part. You staple the little permit tags to the ends of the loads, so everything is legal. The ladies compliment you on the great job you did.

Maybe I'm being *paranoid* here, but every now and then, I wonder if it's not actually the *women* that run things on this world.

Your stuffed coyote didn't hold up well through all the weather of the last year and a half, and he's starting to look *real* raggedy. Apparently, there are *care requirements* for stuffed critters that simply eluded you. You

    a. follow the advice of the many and return him to nature, so his spirit can be free;

    b. take him to one of them taxidermy guys for a tune-up; or

    c. toss him into the dumpster at your ex-employer's place.

Having decided to return Spot to the wild, you position him on top of a hill, surrounded by dirt bike trails to let him have some fun. Knowing that most people have never been close to a coyote, you figure this will be *enlightening*.

Two months later, you return to the place where you left Spot to find that he's *no longer* there. You

    a. figure that Spirit took Spot to coyote heaven,

b. assume that someone adopted Spot, or

c. wonder if Spirit brought Spot back to life.

You're attending a Hunkapi ceremony for adoption and naming for a friend of yours. The elder doing the adopting announces that your friend's Indian name is now "Stands Like Buffalo." This is *the* most flatulent guy you know. You

a. quietly ask the person next to you, "Shouldn't that be '*Farts* Like Buffalo'?";

b. loudly ask the elder, "Hey! Shouldn't that be '*Farts* Like Buffalo'?"; or

c. holler, "Hey! His name outta be '*Green* Cloud'!"

In the old days, people were first named according to a vision the medicine person had (yeah, sometimes they were *women!*), which accounts for names like "Jumping Deer" and "Gnawing Beaver" (along with all the jokes about the two dogs). When people came of age, their names were usually changed to reflect the way they conducted themselves, thus names like "Shoots His Enemies" or "Sits On His Butt."

CHAPTER 11

Hunting Tips

You're deer hunting, using the ammo your dad reloaded eleven years ago. The buck you're aiming at is three hundred yards away. Your first shot is a little low, startling the deer. As the buck leaps and starts to run, you squeeze the trigger and hear, "*Click*," so you drop the hammer again. "*Click*." Ejecting that shell, you fire your remaining bullet. You believe you hit the deer, but it's still running. Following the critter, you find it one hundred yards from where you hit it, leaning against a tree, wheezing and looking at you. You examine your options:

a. Since you're out of ammo, do you club the deer with the vintage rifle you're carrying?
b. Do you wait and hope the deer falls over all by itself?
c. Do you pull out your trusty Marine Corps survival knife (the K- Bar, not those new ones) and jump on it like Tarzan?

After you've stopped the bleeding from where the deer gored your leg with an antler—as you were jumping on its neck—you realize you're over a mile from the road. You

a. choose to carry the deer fireman style with the rifle hanging off its horns,

b. the critter, or

c. leave the deer and go after a horse to haul it with.

As you set the buck down by the side of the road—where your vehicle *used* to be—it dawns on you that there's a problem. Apparently, your wife got tired of waiting while you were out tromping around in the forest and drove off. You

a. pick up the deer and start walking again,

b. sit on the deer and stick out your thumb when a vehicle approaches, or

c. build a fire and start making jerky.

While sitting on a log, wearing your "glow in the dark, see me from *space*" orange hunting vest and matching hat, a bullet strikes next to you— sending bark flying. Do you

a. jump up, wave your arms, and shout, "Don't shoot! I'm a *horse*";

b. dive behind the log, hoping you're on the *correct* side, and scream, "Friendly!"; or

c. dive behind the log then return fire?

Whatever happened to people actually *knowing* what they were shooting at? My grandpa used to hallucinate while hunting and see horns then accidentally shoot does, but at least he was *positive* he'd been shooting a *deer*.

Those people running around all camouflaged, hunting (deer?) with assault rifles makes a strong case for bow hunting!

You're hunting, and it's been raining for three days, so *everything* is muddy. The game warden pulls up and motions for you to open the passenger door of his truck. He has a topo map spread across his seat and asks you to tell him the *most direct* way to get to where he wants to go. Do you

a. laugh at him for being lost,

    b.   show him and tell him that *you* couldn't get over that route yesterday because of the mud,

    c.   show him then wave goodbye and enjoy the show through your binoculars, or

    d.   be a nice guy and suggest an alternate route?

In the South, deer season, hog season, and squirrel season occur all at the same time, and you have to use a shotgun for hunting any of those critters. You're only allowed three shells in your weapon at any given time.

Since gray squirrels are pretty small, the shotgun BBs for shooting them are also small. The BBs required for shooting javelina are much larger since those tuskers are a *lot* bigger than squirrels and tough as buffalo. Hunting deer, on the other hand, requires "pumpkin balls" (solid lead slugs).

So as you're diddy bopping through the woods in some areas, that type of topography would be called "a *jungle*," but in the South, they call that "the woods." Looking for elusive squirrels, wild pigs, and ferocious deer, you have to figure out *how* to have the correct shells in the gun for the particular critter you encounter.

Having spotted a "squirrel tree" up ahead (a large tree where several squirrels have nests), you load up on squirrel shot. As you're sneaking up on the squirrels, four javelinas walk out in front of you, 90 feet ahead. Do you

    a.   completely lose your mind and pop all three of the squirrel shotshells at them;

    b.   calmly and quietly eject the squirrel shot then load the hog shot and fire; or

    c.   get excited, rapidly eject the squirrel shot, load the hog shot, then wonder where the javelina go?

After firing all three squirrel shotshells at them, the pigs turn and charge you *rapidly*. You've obviously pissed them off *severely*. Do you

    a.   boldly stand and reload,

b. break and run, or

c. break and run while reloading?

Realizing that the javelinas are going to catch you *before* you finish reloading, you

a. stop, pull out your survival knife, and become a legend;

b. drop the shotgun and climb the nearest tree; or

c. try to climb the tree with the shotgun in your hands.

As you're sitting in the tree, watching the javelina take turns chewing the wooden stock off your shotgun, you wonder how they managed to work out the rotation of having two of them guard you—doing a *very* convincing "I'm a pissed off hog with three-inch tusks!" display while the other two reduce your weapon to steel and wood chips. Then they switch. What is the signal for them to trade places?

Satisfied that your (now useless) shotgun won't irritate them again, the pigs collectively express their opinion of you then leave.

You're duck hunting with a buddy across a small pond from one another. Your partner starts blasting away at some mallards, and you realize the shotgun BBs are bouncing off the water, hitting *you*. You

a. quickly develop a lower profile and wait for him to stop shooting,

b. get low and move around the pond to his position, or

c. shoot back.

Once you've stress-tested the rubber recoil pad of your shotgun against your buddy's forehead, you

a. *loudly* suggest that he attends a hunter's safety course soon,

b. remind him that the manufacturer of his weapon *strongly* recommends that *only* persons with an IQ *larger* than their shoe size actually be authorized to use the weapon, or

    c.   toss his shotgun into the pond to see whether it's as full of air as his head seems to be.

You hear the sounds of a *lot* of weapon fire coming over the ridge from where you are. This is rapid-fire stuff that sounds like a *major* firefight. Do you

    a.   prudently move in the *opposite* direction,
    b.   allow your curiosity to get the better of you and stroll over to see what all the noise is about, or
    c.   cautiously move over the ridge to see what's going on?

From a place of concealment on the other side of the ridge, you see two guys with AK-47s firing clip after clip, *full auto*, at a running elk over a *mile* from their position (*and* uphill!). You

    a.   spot the elk with your binoculars to see if it's actually in danger from these two,
    b.   sit back to enjoy the show, or
    c.   radio the game warden to come scoop these idiots out of the forest before they shoot *each other*.

A tough call. While guys like that are *rarely* a danger to the game animals, they do present a very serious threat to other humans, as well as most livestock in the vicinity—even the ones the ranchers spray paint *large* letters on (cow).

My rule of thumb is if you ain't engaged in actual *warfare*, you probably don't require fully automatic weapons. Call me a sissy, but I just don't see the need.

CHAPTER 12

Roadkill—Handling Precautions

You're riding in your buddy's car when the truck in front of you hits a deer and keeps on going. The deer is lying motionless on the side of the road. You

    a. crack open another lite beer and think, "Wow, what a waste of meat!" as you drive by;

    b. bounce off the dashboard as your partner slams on the brakes, screaming, "Roadkill!"; or

    c. slap your buddy and holler, "Free venison!"

Five minutes after you've helped your friend load the deer into the trunk of his car, you begin to hear noises from the rear of the vehicle. Shortly thereafter, you definitely hear and *feel* movement from the trunk.

Obviously, that deer wasn't nearly as dead as you'd thought. Do you

    a. try to ignore the noise and continue to drive home—where you can shoot the deer when you open the trunk;

    b. stop and start *real* fast several times, hoping to stun the deer again;

    c.   jump out of the car and shoot through the trunk lid several times in a wide dispersal to finish the critter off; or

    d.   pop the trunk open, grab the tire iron, and smack the deer between the eyes?

Okay, time for a reality check.

Where *exactly* is the gas tank of your buddy's car? The answer is probably, "Right *under* the deer's butt." So shooting the deer might not be such a great idea. But maybe if you get down real low, then line up the shot so the bullet goes through the back seat? Is your friend willing to risk the vintage eight-track player in the dash? Those things are pretty hard to come by these days.

When you pop open the trunk lid, the deer jumps out, knocking your buddy on his butt, and runs *directly* toward the neighbor's house. Do you

    a.   start shooting as fast as you can work the bolt on your friend's rifle;

    b.   decide not to risk shooting the neighbor's house and watch the deer run away;

    c.   move sideways, hoping to line up a better shot; or

    d.   forget the deer and check to see if your buddy is still alive?

Later, as you're having a cheeseburger rather than venison steaks, your friend is saying that it's probably a *good* thing the deer didn't have any horns when it headbutted him in the chest. It could have gotten *real* ugly!

You miss most of his reminiscing as you crack open another lite beer and ponder the idea of starting a "deer relocation" program.

You're rolling along, and you spot an owl that's crashed and burned on the road. Do you

    a.   pick it up, thinking of your nontraditional friends who can use the bird's wings for their ceremonies;

b. drive on by, knowing that your traditional relatives would be *horrified* if you brought it around them; or

c. check to see if it's too far gone to panfry?

Same scenario, but you've discovered a downed red-tailed hawk. Do you

a. promptly scoop it up, knowing it'll make an excellent ceremonial gift for *any* of your relatives;

b. grab it, intending to bogart it for yourself;

c. call the fish and game people like you're *supposed* to do; or

d. keep driving?

Keeping feathers and parts of raptors (hawks, eagles, etc.) is actually *illegal* (not to be confused with "ill eagle" or "dead eagle") and can *really* be a serious *pain* if you're not a card-carrying Indian. Many non-Indian people do use them for the ceremony in a *good* way, so that's an issue that needs to be addressed with an open mind and a clear heart.

While driving down the road, an oncoming vehicle hits a deer, knocking it into your windshield, which breaks your window, sending 150 pounds of shredded venison and glass fragments into your face. The exploding airbags are an extra treat! Your truck is *totaled*. After you ascertain that you're not seriously injured, you

a. decide that since your *truck* is more heavily damaged than the other guy's truck. You claim "roadkill rights" for all the venison;

b. call your insurance agent and ask him if he's got a recipe for deer tacos; or

c. call the *other* guy's insurance agent and *demand* a recipe for deer stew.

You see a dead skunk along the road. Do you

a. drive *way* around it to avoid the smell,

b. carefully scoop it into a trash bag to leave at the home of someone who owes you money, or

c. skin it and make a *fine* (but stinky) hat out of it?

After you've scooped the critter into your trash bag, you realize this skunk was only *stunned*. Now it's flopping around in the bag, and you figure it's only a (*short*) matter of time before it tears the bag open with those claws it has. Do you

a. quickly drop the bag and run away,

b. smack the bag several times to finish the critter off, or

c. talk soothingly to the critter to calm it into being friends?

You're at the grocery store, buying several cans of tomato juice because you've been sprayed by a *very* pissed off skunk (who apparently wasn't feeling all *that* friendly after being hit by a car then jammed into a trash bag). People are backing away whenever you get within 8 feet of them.

At the cash register, the store clerk looks like she feels *trapped* and may puke at any moment. All the other customers have decided to continue shopping at the *back* of the store. Do you

a. toss *more* than enough money at her as you *run* through the check stand and keep going;

b. timidly apologize as you pay for the juice;

c. smile and ask if she'd like to buy a skunk; or

d. tell her, "New cologne. Like it?"

CHAPTER 13

Social Customs—How to Avoid the Faux Pas

You're at a church gathering when one of the deacons calls for attention and says, "Let's all bow our heads and pray." As soon as everything quiets down, everyone *clearly* hears the woman in the corner, talking on her cell phone. She's completely oblivious to the sudden silence. You

    a. clear your throat *really* loud,

    b. crack *up* laughing! or

    c. check to make *sure your* phone is turned off.

While greeting a group of people, a man with a European accent kisses you on *both* cheeks. You

    a. gently place both your hands behind his neck then headbutt him,

    b. go with the *Euro-flow* and return the cheek kiss, or

    c. turn *bright* red and shake his hand.

During introductions at a party, a man *without* a European accent kisses you on the *lips*. You

   a.   do a very convincing Darth Vader imitation, lifting the guy off the floor by his *neck*;
   b.   freak out and bite his lips off; or
   c.   pull back and calmly tell him you're *not comfortable* with that.

During introductions at a party, a woman you've never met kisses you on the lips. You

   a.   gently pull back, smile, and ask, "Do I *know* you?";
   b.   place both your hands behind her head and try to suck her *lungs* out; or
   c.   pull back and calmly tell her you're *not comfortable* with that.

Have you ever noticed how people hug? There's the traditional "manly hug" where two guys *quickly* embrace, slap each other on the back *twice*, then rapidly back up two and a half feet.

CHAPTER 14

Feng Shui—Survival Tips

Your wife calls the feng shui adviser for redecorating ideas. Do you

    a. go deer hunting for the next *three* years;

    b. quietly set up an ambush, so your wife never actually sees the feng shui person;

    c. meekly sit on the porch and wait until your wife sends you and your credit card to Home Depot; or

    d. answer, "Feng *what*? Ah hell, *no*!"

You and your wife are walking through your house, listening to the feng shui lady's suggestion, "This bathroom needs to be *purple* to seat your wealth, but you *must* keep the door closed so the plumbing in here doesn't drain the wealth out of your home. You won't be able to use *this* bed [the captain's bed you *love* because of the drawers under it]. It doesn't allow energy to flow under it. You'll have to relocate your bedroom to the far [opposite] corner of the house [as far away from the bathroom as you can get without being in the back yard!]. Oh, and I'd recommend painting your new bedroom rose or some soft shade of pink."

This goes on for ninety minutes. Your wife is using a small, handheld tape recorder so she doesn't miss *anything*.

Meanwhile, you're wondering if anyone *else* has noticed that this appears to be a communist plot inspired to force American guys to spend vast amounts of money on redecorating, thus driving the middle-class proletariat into bankruptcy, allowing the fat-cat communist leaders to walk in and buy America for a few measly yen.

Of course, it could be just *fear* of *change*, inspiring a wildly paranoid moment.

While you are aware that Home Depot has an interior decorating center—where they have pink blinds—you've never actually *been* in that part of the store before. You don't personally know anyone who has.

You're about to explore uncharted territory.

So after you've painted your new bedroom "Lovable" (a dark coral pink that's actually tolerable) and hung the pink blinds, you get to help pick new furniture and accessories for the room. Everything for this room *must* be in matching pairs (two nightstands, two lamps, etc.) to represent the balanced nature of your relationship. Do you

   a. point out that they have "matching pairs" (in pink, blue, or black!) down at the truck store to hang under the back of your truck? A pair of those would look *perfect* over the bed!
   b. buy one of those "truck accessories" to put under one leg of the bed as a sign of defeat;
   c. humbly push the shopping cart along as your wife spends your money on stuff you didn't know existed; or
   d. enthusiastically embrace all the changes, hoping the feng shui stuff actually works?

The process of rearranging/remodeling goes like this. First, you have to decide *what* to move *where* to get it out of the way. Then you have to *clean* whatever it is you're going to move. Once that's done, you have to clean the spot where you're moving the preselected object *to*, and *finally*, you move it. Then, of course, you have to clean the spot you just vacated.

This process is repeated over and over until the job is done, or you die from exhaustion—whichever occurs first.

Part of the larger focus of feng shui is to reduce the amount of clutter in the home. Somewhere along the way—with all the shuffling of stuff—it becomes *painfully* obvious that there's more crap than places to *put* it. That's the practical aspect of feng shui.

So it's time for a trip to the secondhand store. In some areas, the thrift stores will actually send a truck to your house to pick up all your "donations." Some of them have very *large* trucks, often with large men (in recovery programs) driving them.

CHAPTER 15
Romance and Feeling Frisky

Your wife is on the other side of the room, folding clothes on the bed. The bed is between you, and you're feeling "frisky." Do you

- a. make what would be in football a *stunning* horizontal dive in an attempt to bite her on the butt;
- b. calmly move around the bed, gently caress her, and softly kiss her neck; or
- c. flop down in the middle of the clothes and ask, "Do ya *wanna?*"

There have been numerous books written on *exactly* that topic, yet *no* one seems to have the perfect, works-every-time answer. Give it your best shot and hope for the best.

You're outside, *heavily* involved in working on your truck, and your wife starts pestering you because *she's* feeling "frisky." Do you

- a. crawl a little further under the truck, so she can't reach you;
- b. start tossing wrenches blindly, over your shoulder, to see if she'll go away; or
- c. immediately stop what you're doing, and start putting greasy handprints ALL over her?

You're at a concert with your wife when you see an old friend walking with a blond you've never seen before. You thought this friend is supposed to be at a different function about then.

You nudge your wife, and she says, "Oh, yeah. That's the gal from that class he's taking. He likes her, but she's a *smoker*."

Your wife goes to get their attention, and your friend introduces the blond.

The blond goes back out into the lobby to smolder, and your friend tells your wife she's wrong. This isn't the woman from the class. This is a woman from the *escort service*. He explains that he wanted some company for this concert and just didn't want to hassle with social stuff. You respond to this:

    a. "Oh, I see. That's…interesting."
    b. "Ah. So what it cost for one of them *rent-a-dates?*"
    c. You respectfully keep a straight face and only grunt, "Uh."

After the concert, your friend and the *rent girl* hop into a stretched limo and disappear. On the other side of town, you encounter the limo again headed toward your friend's place with the *rent-a-chick* still inside. You

    a. make three hundred jokes in rapid succession and laugh *hysterically*;
    b. struggle *real* hard to fight down the temptation to call his place forty-five minutes later; or
    c. laugh till you choke, then spend the rest of the night giggling like a teenager.

Sometimes, a situation can be perceived as perfectly acceptable in a particular setting and viewed as *way* off-the-wall in a different setting. It's kind of *how* you look at it and *where* you're standing while looking—another of those subtle social things.

You're single (or at least *acting* like it), and you see a *very* attractive person that you'd *really* like to be intimate with. Do you

    a.   walk up, introduce yourself, and ask, "Do ya *wanna?*";

    b.   attempt to make small talk even though you've *never* been good at it;

    c.   plan ahead and have yourself surgically altered so you *can* lick your eyebrows; or

    d.   quickly jot down a beautiful poem and give it to her, explaining that you're not good at talking?

All these ideas have merit and *have* been field-tested. It all depends on who you believe yourself to be and how drunk you are. Stupid ideas *always* make a *lot* more sense after a few whiskey sours.

You wake up with an ugly hangover, staring at a ceiling you don't recognize and realize you're trapped (in a strange bed) *under* one of *the* homeliest people you've ever seen. Do you

    a.   close your eyes and hope for death;

    b.   cautiously extricate yourself, hoping you don't wake this beast;

    c.   think of it as "charity work" and go back to sleep; or

    d.   be grateful that *someone* thought enough of you to drag *you* home?

You've met an attractive woman while doing spiritual things in the community. She makes it *abundantly* clear that she'd like to get to know you *intimately.* Both of you are in a relationship with other people. Do you

    a.   take the moral high road and make it *clear* that you're unavailable,

    b.   take the low road and see what she has to offer,

    c.   ask if her boyfriend is going to be participating, or

    d.   ask if she minds your wife joining in?

You've met an attractive man while doing spiritual things in the community. He makes it *very* clear that he'd like to be intimate with you. Both of you are involved with someone else. Do you

    a. take the moral high road and make it *clear* that you're unavailable,
    b. take the low road and see what he has to offer,
    c. ask if his wife is going to be participating, or
    d. ask if he minds your husband joining in?

Same story—different perspectives. Any answers changed? Sometimes, we tend to have differing opinions of what's "appropriate," depending on who's doing the looking and who's being looked at. These days, that old *double standard* doesn't wash as easily as it used to.

You get back from a party, and you're all *revved* up, but your date ain't interested. She says, "No!" just before she passes out. Do you

    a. take her home and see that she's safe;
    b. figure, "Ah, what the hell?" and go for the gusto; or
    c. call her people and wrap her in a blanket on the couch?

You get home from a party, and you're all *revved* up, but your wife ain't interested. She says, "No!" just before she passes out. Do you

    a. tuck her into bed and go take a shower;
    b. figure, "Ah, what the hell?" and go for the gusto; or
    c. drag your wife into the shower to wake her up, so you can ask again?

Everybody *should* know that it's *not* okay to jump on your date when they're passed out. It's against the law. People go to jail for that in some places for a *very* long time.

So let's see a show of hands! How many of you thought it was *okay* to jump on your wife after she's passed out? Here's a tidbit of information for you. In many states, it's against the law to have relations with your *wife* after she says, "No."

How would *you* feel if you were passed out (and oddly enough *wanted* to be left alone!), then someone took advantage of you? Picture yourself being tossed in jail for drinking, then having "Bruno" want to play with you as you pass out.

General rule of thumb, when in doubt, *don't*.

Your wife brings you a sample pack of Viagra. Do you

 a. take two and start ripping your clothes off *before* the pills take effect;
 b. toss them in the nightstand drawer with the ones your doctor gave you;
 c. follow the directions and smoothly ease into "passionate mode"; or
 d. take the hint, toss the pills over your shoulder, and go *directly* into "passionate mode"?

Option "C" would give you time to light some candles to create ambiance and maybe generate some epic memories.

You're watching football on TV, and your wife decides it's time to pay attention to *her*. She stands in front of the television and starts to do a striptease. Do you

 a. lean way over in your chair, trying to see *around* her;
 b. throw popcorn at her and yell, "Down in front!";
 c. point the remote at *her* while pushing the button, hoping it'll make her go away; or
 d. stand up and start caressing her while watching the game over her shoulder?

Of course, there *are* guys that'd just turn off the game and help with the striptease. No, no! It's *true*! I've *seen* it!

Well, I didn't stick around to watch how it *ended* (that would have been *rude!*), but it looked like the football game was *history*.

The Winston Cup is on, and your *favorite* driver is running a *close* second with seven laps to go. Your wife comes into the room in a *very* nice, see- through negligee and plants herself in your lap. You

    a. freak *out*, dump her on the floor, and move to another chair;

    b. quickly hit "record mode" on the VCR then give her your full *undivided* attention; or

    c. move her off you, explaining that there are only seven laps to go—*then* you'll be *all* hers.

You've been working overtime but left work *early* so you could catch the Daytona 500. You *rush* home to watch the race and find your living room— where the 52-inch HDTV is (with surround sound!)— *full* of women, having what appears (at first glance) to be a Tupperware party. The race *starts* in two minutes. You

    a. lose your mind and toss everybody *out*,

    b. turn on the TV in the bedroom then ask your wife if she and all the ladies could relocate to the patio,

    c. turn on the race in the living room and *try* to ignore the chaos it creates.

While in the process of running errands around town, you become aware that someone is following you. Do you

    a. call 911 on your cell phone,

    b. stop at a phone booth *then* call 911,

    c. slip into "James Bond mode" and start driving erratically as fast as you can, or

    d. ignore it?

When you reach the "Cheapo's Depot" tool place and get out of your vehicle, the guy who's been following you also gets out. He tells you how attractive he thinks you are and asks if you'd like to go have coffee. Do you

    a.   break and run, screaming;

    b.   politely point out that you're married and *straight*;

    c.   go into a homophobic mode and freak *all* the way out; or

    d.   if this looks like your kind of guy, decide to overlook the stalker aspects of this situation and accept?

It sounds kinda scary, but I suppose you have to be there to decide. At least keep your cell phone on speed dial.

You're at the airport in a city you've never been to before with a six-hour layover, and you're on an *extremely* tight budget. You notice that a beautiful woman keeps looking at you and smiles whenever you make eye contact. Do you

    a.   remind yourself that you're married and focus on your book,

    b.   wander around the terminal to amuse yourself,

    c.   smile and point to your wedding ring, or

    d.   walk over to see if she'll buy you lunch?

An innocent lunch in public can be just an innocent lunch and some pleasant company. However, the potential for weirdness is definitely present. Even a thousand miles from home, a thing like that can bite you on the butt! It's sort of like bathing in gasoline and playing with matches.

You get into bed, and your wife screams at you for having cold feet. You

    a.   offer to warm them between her thighs,

    b.   ask her to rub them to warm them, or

    c.   put your boots back on and get into bed again.

You slide into bed, and your wife tells you your *butt* is cold. You

    a.   press it *firmly* against her side to warm it,
    b.   rip off a *big* fart to warm it, or
    c.   put some long johns on.

While attempting to be intimate *before* your eyes have adjusted to the dark, you go through several spastic and somewhat *painful* contacts with your lover, leaving both of you with fat lips and what may become a black eye. You

    a.   decide to quit *before* you need an ambulance;
    b.   do *first* aid and start over with more light; or
    c.   light a candle, kiss each other's wounds, and start again.

The phone rings while you're making love. You *cannot* reach the phone from where you are. Do you

    a.   ignore it and *try* to stay focused on what you're doing;
    b.   answer it? It *could* be important;
    c.   freak *out*, answer it, and tell the person just *what* they interrupted; or
    d.   be *really* glad you don't have one of those *view screens* like on sci- fi movies?

CHAPTER 16

Critters in Your Yard

You have wild rabbits living in your backyard (the cute cotton tail-type, not those mangy jackrabbits), and you *love* to watch them hop around the yard, grazing on your weeds. They're really good about not eating the things you plant—except for the raspberry vines. Those things seem to be *irresistible* to the bunnies. Do you

    a. try speaking to the bunnies to work out a compromise,
    b. revisit your childhood and have roasted bunny, or
    c. put chicken wire around the new raspberry plants?

After you discover the tops of your new raspberry plants chewed off (thus killing the vines) because the rabbits pushed over the frames of chicken wire, you begin to seriously rethink the whole "cute bunny" concept. Do you

    a. have another chat with the rabbits, "*Bad* bunny! Leave those vines alone";
    b. break out the old crossbow and warm up the BBQ; or
    c. fence off the entire area where you wanted raspberries?

Three out of the four bunnies obviously felt chastised and left the raspberries alone. I put up a two-foot chicken wire fence around the berry patch to keep that one *miscreant* bunny out.

It's spring, and the birds are pairing off and nesting everywhere. The sparrows seem to be comfortable building nests in every little cranny they can find. There's one pair of quail that just doesn't seem to get it. They're like those Visa card signs—they're *everywhere* you want to go.

It's a thrill to open your front door and have a pair of quail fly out of the flower bed to scare the hell out of you!

Throughout the winter, there's been *one* chucker hanging out with the quail—a *wannabe* quail. He stood out like a dog at a cat show! He was the size of a *big* chicken. The quail all accepted him until they started to pair off for mating. Suddenly, the difference *mattered*.

It was like that old cartoon, where the character is big and dumb. "Duh, which way did they go? Hey, wait up!" Then the female quail *fled* in all directions.

Another example of evolution at work. It appears *his* gene pool is going dry up. Besides, if he *did* catch a quail, what the hell would we *call* it? A chail? A quacker?

That'd be right up there with the mythic "jackalope."

You're driving down the road, and a rabbit starts to cross in front of you. Do you

    a.   stop and let the bunny cross,
    b.   swerve and *hope* you miss it,
    c.   swerve and hope you hit it?

You can kinda tell what people's attitudes are by the location of the flat bunnies (and *how* flat they actually are!). The bunny haters will go *all* the way to the curb (and sometimes *over!*) to make a kill. Usually, those rabbits are *extremely* flat! I think it's them big truck tires.

As you're driving down a backcountry dirt road, you spot a *large* snake crossing the road. Do you

    a. keep on cruising,
    b. stop and let it cross safely, or
    c. jump out with your Buck knife and grab up the main ingredient for some *snake stew*?

I guess the answer to that one depends on whether you *know* from experience that snake "tastes *just* like chicken," or you are one of those people that eat flavored tofu. Of course, there *are* some omnivores who believe in preserving nature (when we're not *hungry*).

Someone in the neighborhood has lost a pet rat, one of those white ones, and it has decided to take up residence in your yard. Rats are not indigenous to your part of the country, but if it finds a playmate, things could quickly get out of hand. Do you

    a. keep an eye on it to see how it'll fit in,
    b. set out a live trap so you can relocate it, or
    c. set out a real trap to be rid of the critter?

While doing an inspection of your irrigation system, you discover that the rat is robbing the quail nests and eating the eggs. You *really* enjoy watching the quail. You

    a. set out several lethal traps to eliminate the rat,
    b. set out poison and hope it doesn't get anything *but* the rat,
    c. go into "Rambo mode" and set up a couple of tiny claymore mines around a fake quail nest to make shredded rat, or
    d. load up on rat shot and go into stalking mode?

After having found the rat *dead* (apparently, the little bastage *choked* to death on a quail bone!), you need to dispose of the carcass. Do you

    a. quietly wrap it in newspaper and toss it in the trash;

b. treat it like a squirrel and *cook* it, drying the skin on your clothesline;

c. hang it from your fence post as a deterrent to any others; or

d. toss it over the fence for the neighbor's lab to play with?

Some ideas just don't work as well as they did back in the old (medieval) days. Also, you could wind up getting *hurt* if anyone found out you'd served them rat meat!

You become aware that you have a squirrel that's taken up residence in your yard. Up to this point in time, you are *positive* that there are *no* squirrels living in your valley (they don't cross mountain ranges). You assume

a. that this is a *spirit*, come to give you a message about gathering the things you need;

b. that someone has unintentionally (or *worse* intentionally) imported a squirrel from a neighboring valley;

c. this is the rat—reincarnated.

You take your assuming to the next level. You figure

a. if this *is* a spirit, it will go away once you've acknowledged its message;

b. since some ecologically retarded person imported this critter, you'll have to wait and see how it's going to fit into the little wildlife zoo you already have going in your yard; or

c. that you need to replace the fake quail nest with a bag of peanuts then rearm the miniature claymores.

Where I come from, tacos with shredded squirrel sounds just fine— certainly a *lot* better than tacos with a shredded *rat*—but again, it's a personal perspective thing. I used to know some Montagnards who would have *loved* that.

The neighbors' cats come into your backyard to hunt the birds you love to watch. You

   a. set out live traps to catch them and take them to animal control,
   b. break out the slingshot for some animal behavioral training, or
   c. break out the .22 rifle using .22 *shorts* so they don't go far (it *is* a residential area after all!).

Personally, I think the slingshot is the best choice. Of course, there are other options, such as using a bow and arrows or a crossbow, and there's always a wide variety of snares if you're one of them Daniel Boone types. I suppose blowguns are also an option, but where would you get any curare?

I've heard that you can call animal control, and they'll actually *bring* you a live trap for problem critters.

On the other hand, I've been *told* that "roof rabbit" tastes *just* like chicken. Anyone (who speaks *English*) know for sure? Got recipes?

CHAPTER 17

Apparel and Other Fashion Statements

You're wearing a navy blue and white pinstripe (long sleeve) button-down shirt with forest camo BDU pants when someone looks at you, takes a step back, and says, "Cheese and *rice*! You dress like a Bohemian!" You respond,

a. "Oh, thanks!";
b. "A Bo-*what*?";
c. "Wow! That sounds *painful*!"; or
d. "Ah man! Is it *contagious*?"

Or my personal favorite response is "I dressed *myself*. Does it look okay?"

Your wife wants to go into town, so you put on a clean T-shirt and roll. Once you get where you're going, your lovely wife notices that your shirt has two half-inch burn holes right in the center of your chest. When ask if you *know* the holes are there, you respond,

a. "Of course. I was *in* this shirt when it was burned";
b. "Oh, wow! Where'd *those* come from?"; or

c. "This shirt was missin' for a couple of weeks. I think them *aliens* musta took it."

Having now noticed the holes, she keeps trying to stick her fingers into them to tear your shirt. Once you realize she means to *destroy* your shirt, you

   a. go back out to your truck to put some duct tape over the holes,
   b. duct tape your wife's hands together, or
   c. bite her fingers every time they get too close.

Some people would say that tearing off your spouse's T-shirt in public is uncivilized behavior, while others seem to think it's perfectly okay as long as the person *under* the T-shirt is visually appealing.

Of course, there *are* those who believe activities like that should only be done in private, between consenting adults.

Okay. So let's see a show of hands! Who'd like to see a T-shirt torn off of a great-looking twenty-something (pick your favorite gender)?

Now let's see the other side of the coin. Who'd like to see a T-shirt torn off a *chubby*, wrinkly old (pick your favorite gender)?

A double standard, eh? The old and wrinkly *never* get equal time. On the other hand, many of the old and wrinkly are young and cute themselves back in the Stone Age.

It must have been tough back then, riding those dinosaurs to go out on dates.

One of your buddies is wearing a pair of jeans that, obviously, are treated to a bath in battery acid—half the backside is *gone*—and he ain't wearing any underwear. One glance and you've already gotten *way* too much information! You

   a. tactfully hand him a roll of duct tape and the Walmart ad for underwear,

    b.   loan him a shirt with *really* long tails, or

    c.   spray gasket adhesive on a shop towel and slap it over his butt.

You're about to go somewhere with a female friend. She tells you, "I have to put on a different pair of pants. These have holes in them." You

    a.   get *real* busy looking for the holes;

    b.   ask, "What holes?"; or

    c.   answer, "Uh."

When she reappears twenty-five seconds later in what looks like the *same* pair of jeans, you

    a.   exclaim, "Wow! That didn't take long!";

    b.   resume looking for holes; or

    c.   answer, "Uh," and move toward the door.

When ask if what makes you decide to choose a particular camo outfit to wear, you

    a.   give a chin nod to indicate the area *behind* the person who asked, use two fingers (coming from your eyes), and point, moving your whole arm in a sweeping motion across the vast forest before you;

    b.   nod your head and ask, "Which *city* are you from?"; or

    c.   answer, "Walmart only had *Mossy Oak*."

You arrive in North Dakota, wearing your "prairie ghost" camo outfit (the *perfect* pattern for Nevada's sagebrush!), to find that you

    a.   stick out like a sore thumb on a *sea* of green!

    b.   look like a clump of sagebrush, *moving* across the grass; or

    c.   can't move without being seen from *space*.

Two hours later, you're being told that the closest drugstore is 33 miles away. You started asking over half an hour ago when you first started to itch *real* bad because the vegetation you used for extra camo turned out to be poison ivy.

Everyone was laughing so hard they couldn't *speak* to answer you.

CHAPTER 18
Self-Help Workshops

You're at a "growth and development" weekend workshop with a bunch of people—some you know, most you don't. Lunchtime rolls around, and everyone has different suggestions on where to go. You're driving with five others. The popular consensus is to go to a health food place. On the way there, you

    a. let everyone know that you do *not* consider *tofu* a food substance;

    b. decide, since you're working on broadening your horizons, you'll go with the flow;

    c. tell everyone you'll drop them off and go down the street to the *authentic* taco stand on the corner; or

    d. stop at the corner market to load up on junk food and scarf it at the health food place.

As you sit—surrounded by clog-wearing salad eaters—you stare in *horror* at the disgusting chunk of tofu on your recycled paper plate, wondering *why* this thing is *moving*. You

    a. start stabbing the tofu with your recycled spork while screaming, "*Die*, you alien monster!";

b.   pretend you're a Klingon and relish the warm squiggly texture;

c.   carefully lift the plate and carry it to the trash, hoping the tofu doesn't leap up and attack your face; or

d.   ask, "Hey is this stuff *supposed* to be movin'?"

During one of the many exercises of the workshop, you're asked to "get angry" while going through a scenario with the person in front of you. You

a.   feel completely awkward and fail to do more than giggle,

b.   step into their "space" while glaring intensely, or

c.   burst out laughing while trying to sound angry.

When told that you're not *angry*, you respond,

a.   "No, but I *could* be!" as you lift him off the floor by the neck;

b.   "I ain't got a *reason* to be angry"; or

c.   "Is there some *point* to this?"

Another exercise is to have one person acting as the "leader" move around the (very *large*) room while doing odd posturing and gestures. The other person is supposed to follow and mimic the leader. During this activity, you

a.   crash and burn doing the duck waddle;

b.   can't picture *anything* in your mind but two orangutans playing; or

c.   fail miserably because the forty other people in the room all look so hysterical you can't focus on what *you're* supposed to be doing.

The next activity places you with a very attractive woman, who asks you, "What are you *feeling* right now?" You

a. *desperately* search your memory for some word *other* than "horny,"
b. stare like a deer in the headlights, or
c. stare *at* her headlights.

Before the workshop, you were told you could bring an exercise ball to sit on. When you arrive, you notice that a friend of yours has brought *the* largest exercise balls you've ever *seen*. Do you

a. innocently say, "Ah man! You've got *big* balls!";
b. announce, "It figures that the *Tantra* guy would have the *biggest* balls in the place!"; or
c. ask, "Are you *compensating* for something?"

Your wife is attending a series of workshops to learn a new healing technique. At one of the classes, her mentor asks her, "Is it the energy work or what? Your hair is *so* much *redder*." She

a. tells you she *should've* answered, "Yeah, it was two bottles of 'prana'";
b. answers, "I think it was a *miracle*!";
c. answers, "Yeah, there's a *lot* to that energy work, eh?"; or
d. stands in silence with her hands together, looking *very* prayerful.

CHAPTER 19

Nostalgia and Classic Cars

While wandering around an antique car show-n-shine, you notice that some of the cars have what are obviously factory colors, and others have flames, deep-candy apple coats, or unusual colors (neon purple?). You

a. ask, "Hey! How come none of these cars have *dents* in 'em?";

b. wonder *why* someone would paint a Dodge Charger flamingo *pink*;

c. think about how *you* used to own cars just like some of these; or

d. wonder if any of these *are* the ones you used to own.

At the car event, they have a bunch (of the survivors) of the bands you liked as a kid, playing all the "oldies." Some of these groups are "tribute bands" (impersonators). You

a. immediately notice that many of the people around you *don't* seem to have aged as well as you did,

b. wonder how the guys in the band *actually* managed to *waddle* up on the stage, or

    c.   realize that the words to your favorite oldie song are *different* now that you're *sober.*

Your favorite band (what's *left* of them) is playing their theme song—which was widely acknowledged as the *anthem* of your generation—and the crowd is going *wild.* Meanwhile, you're thinking of the rewrite you did of this song, which, considering the thirty-plus years that have elapsed, needed to be rephrased to more accurately reflect the current lifestyles of the baby boomers. You called it, "Born to be lethargic." When you attempt to share your wonderful bit of entertaining wisdom, you

    a.   find yourself blocked by what you *thought* was a *large* statue of Adonis in a "security" T-shirt;

    b.   try to bribe the security kid but quickly discover he only speaks three words. "No. Go away!"; or

    c.   look at the event's brochure and notice the band's website then e- mail your "masterpiece" to them.

Oddly, you never get a response to your e-mail.

It looked to me like a person could make a *lot* of money at those events if he could find a line of *truly* natural-looking hairpieces with *ponytails* to sell there. The baseball cap vendors always look like "bald-guy headquarters."

Do I need to develop a bit more empathy for the follicly challenged?

Your wife's grandpa has a 1953 Ford pickup (the fiftieth-anniversary model!) in his backyard. When you ask about it, he tells you he'd like to get $150 for it, but since the motor is blown, he'll take the best offer you're willing to make. You

    a.   pawn your firstborn *son* to get the $150 and buy the truck *before* Grandpa sobers up,

    b.   buy it and start getting it ready to drag home, or

    c.   replace all the tires then drag it through the car wash on the way home.

CHAPTER 20

VA, Indian Health, and Other Fairy Tales

One of your relatives was in the war and just *didn't* seem to be able to move beyond it. Every time you see him, you get to hear the same old war stories *again*. You

    a. help him get a job at the VFW, doing quality control on all their hard liquor;

    b. get him to be a volunteer at the VA, where he can talk to other vets (who *can't* get away from him); or

    c. talk him into joining the foreign legion of some *other* country.

While you're at the VFW, you realize that the mixed drinks are *really* inexpensive. On the other hand, you'd need *earplugs* to be able to tolerate the "bull factor." You have to weigh the value of cheap drinks against the cost and hassle of a bucket of earplugs. Inexpensive ain't always *cheap*.

Your children ask you what you did in the "Army" (to a seven-year-old, *all* branches of the military are "the Army.") You answer,

a. "I was a cook on a battleship";
b. "I was a soldier in the infantry"; or
c. "I dug holes and drank a *lot* of beer."

Your teenager asks you what you did in "the war." You answer,

a. "I worked in a field medical unit";
b. "I hiked around the jungle, wasted a *lot* of ammo on things I couldn't see, smoked weed, and *hoped* I wouldn't get shot";
c. "I fueled jets on an aircraft carrier, off the coast of a country we couldn't even *see*;" or
d. "I walked around, looking for people who were shouting at everyone around them while pointing at things and *shot* them."

I always thought it was ironic how what you *wanted* to be in the military and what you actually wound up *being* were usually two different things. One of my all-time favorite authors used to say that the military had two very *obscure* departments that invariably had an obvious effect on military personnel: *the practical jokes department* and *the fairy godmother department.*

Sometimes, these different forces balance and factor each other out. A classic example would be when a person enlists with an "aviation guarantee" (he wanted to be an aircraft electrician), and he's sent to jump school for airborne training. *This individual is afraid of heights.* After screaming *real* loud, refusing to jump, and tossing the jumpmaster out of the airplane, the military sends the man to a school where he's trained to *spray paint* aircraft—almost a balance.

Maybe I'm just getting cynical. It's one of the things I really liked about Robert A. Heinlein.

You're an active military stationed in Southeast Asia. You (finally) get a chance for some *regional* R&R (can't go back to the US), so you decide to go where you can actually have some fun *without* being accosted by MPs at every corner. You go to Bangkok. Just outside the city are some of *the* most beautiful temples in the world. They're still on your list of things to see.

After drinking way too much rice beer, you decide that you're King Kong, the "*baddest* of the *bad*," and jump into a Thai boxing ring to prove your kung fu prowess. The fact that these people do this every day for a *living* seems to have eluded you at the moment. You find yourself facing a man you think of as an *elder* because he appears to be at least nine hundred years old. He's 5 feet tall, weighs *maybe* 85 pounds, with *long* white hair and wrinkles *all* over. You

- a. bow, salute, and decide you're going to take it *easy* on the old guy;
- b. choose to fight someone a few centuries younger; or
- c. go for the gusto.

As you approach the old man, he shows you a few kung fu stances you've never *seen* before then proceeds to *run* up the front of you, dance around on your shoulders for a minute while gently kicking you on *both* sides of your head and run down the back of you, *laughing*. You

- a. get angry and *attack* this guy with everything you've got;
- b. have an epiphany and realize you're *grossly* outmatched; or
- c. decide to be respectful, let the old guy have some fun, and *hope* it doesn't hurt *too* much.

You realize this old man is *obviously* a master as he continues to *play* with you despite your *best* efforts to represent yourself, making the crowd roar with laughter. You

- a. get angry and make a complete *idiot* of yourself,
- b. continue to give it your best shot while having fun, or
- c. go with the flow until you're too worn out to continue.

Back at the hotel, you do "quality control" on twelve more bottles of beer, thus causing you to lose interest in *all* the bar girls and decide to call it a night.

Some time the next day, you stumble down the stairs to be greeted by tall, *round*-eyed White people, one of whom says, "G'day, mate!" You

    a. feel the compass in your head spin around *three times* then fall forward into your face,

    b. figure you're *sleepwalking* and crawl back up the stairs, or

    c. blink several times and *demand* to see the wizard (thinking you *must* be in Oz).

Sydney, Australia, has some beautiful attractions. They're still on your list of things to see *also*. It seems that your friends in the Australian SAS thought it would be big yucks to transport you to Sydney while you were passed out. So you

    a. go with the flow,

    b. hop on the first flight back to your duty station, or

    c. test drive a few pints of ale.

The Australians talk you into "boxin' wi' a 'roo," and you find yourself in a boxing ring, facing what looks like a *huge* mouse. You've never been this close to a kangaroo before. You

    a. make the same mistake *again* and decide to "take it easy" on this critter,

    b. pull out your K-Bar and see just how cute this rodent is on the *inside*, or

    c. get your butt kicked again and provide *loads* of humorous entertainment.

You're a vet, and people keep telling you to go to the VA for medical help, but you *vividly* remember all the buddies you had who experienced "medical weirdness" in those places (i.e., having a *leg* removed *instead* of the *appendix*), and you just can't bring yourself to go there while you're conscious.

You have to go visit a close friend in the VA hospital. While there, you find

    a. your buddy has been misplaced and can't be located;

    b. your buddy is sitting in a wheelchair next to the nurse's station when the nurse tells you, "I'm sorry, he's not here. Your friend checked himself out and went home"; or

    c. your buddy is trying to climb out the window of his room, anxiously mumbling, "They're tryin' to *kill* me! They gave me a little pink pill, and now they're tryin' to..."

You go to the US Health hospital in a large city for your Indian Health Service. Most of the health care workers you encounter do *not* speak English. You

    a. dip into your old bag of *pidgin* English you used in the military,

    b. start drawing pictures on the tablet you brought, or

    c. speak *very* loud and s-l-o-w-l-y.

Immediately, you realize your pidgin *ain't* going to do the trick since you're *not* looking for a bar, the local black market, or a brothel.

Drawing pictures of anatomy can be pretty frustrating even if you're a *great* artist.

Sign language is generally the best way to wade through those difficult moments when communication has developed *truly hemorrhoidal* qualities.

You're in a military hospital for an exam because you have flat feet. Two Navy doctors (who both *claim* to be podiatrists) are examining your feet. They make you stand up on their table. One of them is trying to stick a dollar bill under the spot your arch *should* be while the other is videotaping the exam. They're *astounded* at how flat your feet are! All the while, they're asking stupid questions like, "How can you *walk*? Does it hurt to *run*? How did you get into the *Marines*? Do flat feet run in your family?" You respond,

a. "I put one foot in front of the other then *lean* forward";
b. "When I'm being *shot* at, it hurts *not* to run!";
c. "There was a war on—maybe you *heard* about it?"; or
d. "Ah, you've heard of the Flathead tribe? My people are the *flatfoots*."

You barely manage to keep a straight face as they write *all* that down. Indian comedy—amazingly, a lot of people just don't get it.

CHAPTER 21
Thrills of Riding

While out riding the open range, your horse steps in a hole and injures its leg. You're *miles* from *anywhere*. You

    a. shoot the horse and walk away;

    b. remove your saddle, turn the critter loose, and tell him he's on his *own*;

    c. remove your saddle then lead the horse while you carry the saddle; or

    d. pick up your horse, across your shoulders (in a fireman's carry), and *pack* him to the vet.

The horse people out there are *freaking out* that someone would even *suggest* abandoning an injured horse! For most of the cowboy types I know, the thought of walking away from an injured horse is *unconscionable*.

You're rolling down the open highway on your "*iron* horse" when the rear cylinder decides to suck a valve. Amid all the noise and smoke, you manage to *safely* maneuver the bike off the road. This motorcycle is as dead as your grandpa's dog, and you're *miles* from *anywhere*. You

    a. shoot the bike and walk away,

    b. pull the keys and your personal gear off the motorcycle and walk away,

    c. start pushing the bike toward the nearest town, or

    d. sit on the scooter and thumb *every* truck and van for a ride to the Harley shop.

Most bikers would *never* abandon their motorcycle. It might be okay for a Honda, but a *Harley* would "grow legs" before the seat got cold.

Interesting comparison, eh? It gets even *more* interesting when you compare the old-time drovers to modern bikers.

You've gone to "play in the sand" with several friends—all of whom are *avid* dirt bikers. After they don all their body armor, they hop on their bikes and disappear over a sand dune. You look around and notice something orange, appearing and disappearing behind the dunes. You

    a. decide to investigate and walk toward the elusive orange thingie;

    b. figure you should stay near the vehicles, maybe the orange object will come to *you*; or

    c. see it popping up all around you and can't decide which way to go.

As you're walking up a sand dune, you suddenly hear a roar, and a VW dune buggy erupts from behind the hill, launching itself *over* your head. You

    a. stand—glued to the spot—then notice the little orange flag above it *after* it lands behind you;

    b. throw yourself to the ground and *continue* to lie there, *hoping* the sand will absorb the extra moisture from where you wet your jeans; or

    c. try to figure out *what* just happened as you scrape the sand out of your eyes.

Having now satisfied your curiosity about the mysterious orange thingie, you

    a.   remember how *wonderful* the view was next to your truck,

    b.   decide to hunt down the maniac in the VW sand rail to tell him *exactly* what you think of his driving, or

    c.   realize you've just found the next thrilling hobby to spend ALL your "spare" money on!

You and your wife have to pick up a friend at the hospital and take him home. Since your friend is injured, your wife rides in the back seat to give him more room. When you drop off your friend, your wife decides to stay in the back seat. Your friend says you look like a *chauffeur*. You

    a.   tell him, "Yeah, I'm drivin' Miss *Lazy*";

    b.   respond, "Yup, I'm drivin' Miss Lazy, oh, I mean, Miss *Daisy*"; or

    c.   grunt and say, "Yeah, *overworked* and *underpaid* with way too much supervision. It's probably a good thing she can't see over the seat, eh?"

You're driving through the parking lot at Walmart, and your wife is giving you directions to the "best" parking space. You're distracted by the old people on your right and the woman with five little kids (all wanting to go in *different* directions!) on the left while keeping an eye on the kid gathering shopping carts 50 feet down the aisle. After you've made three laps around the parking lot, your wife gets agitated and, therefore, *louder*. You

    a.   ask your wife if *she'd* like to drive,

    b.   distract her by asking her to hand you something that's *under* her seat, or

    c.   turn up the radio *really* loud.

Same scenario, but with a teenaged daughter added. Your daughter gets agitated and yells, "Stop, and let me *out*! I'll walk!" You

a. yell at her, "Shut *up!*" and continue driving;
b. instantly recognize the *blessing* you've just been given and let her out; or
c. tune the radio to a *country* station and turn it up really loud.

You're cruising down a two-lane highway surrounded by cotton fields for miles and miles. Your Harley is heavily loaded (with everything you own!), in addition to your lady and all *her* stuff. You come up behind a slow- moving motor home. There's no oncoming traffic, so you start to pass. As you pull even with the cab of the motor home, the old guy driving it looks at you and makes a face like he's just sucked on a lemon then speeds up. He's going faster than the speed limit now, so you drop back behind him. He slows down again. Do you

a. pass the motor home,
b. pull up to ask the old guy if there's a *problem*, or
c. settle into the old guy's slipstream and kick your scooter in neutral?

As you pull out (again) to pass the motor home, the sour-faced fossil speeds up once more. Having enjoyed this scenario for way too long, you twist the throttle, figuring you can outrun this mobile farmhouse, but the old guy keeps pace with you. When your speedometer reaches 100 mph, you see a black dot up ahead (in your lane), rapidly growing larger. The geezer's motor is knocking loudly and starting to smoke as you realize the black dot is a highway patrol cruiser.

Old guy's wife is screaming at him as you see the highway patrolman has just realized you're about to hit the front of his cruiser. You're doing 110 *mph* now. Do you

a. decide to take your chances with the barbed wire fence and cotton field,
b. try to coax your iron horse to go just a *little* faster, or

   c. hit the brakes and drop back behind the lunatic in the motor home?

After squeezing between the mobile retirement home and the highway patrol cruiser, you check your rearview mirror and see the cruiser slewing sideways, attempting to get turned around. You're still rolling along at 110 mph, and you have to pee *severely*. You

   a. start looking for a place to stop,
   b. slow down and try to pee over your leg, or
   c. stop and go pee while waiting for the state trooper to show up.

As you're explaining the situation to the cop, the motor home limps past. The motor is knocking very loudly while *thick* black smoke rolls out from under the hood. This vehicle looks like it was hit by an RPG! The geezer honks and flips you off.

The nice highway patrol officer shakes his head and reduces the ticket from reckless driving (a *felony*) to *careless* driving—then tells you to "drive safe."

CHAPTER 22

Moving and Other Social Headaches

I't's time to move. You've bought a new house, and it's *finally* ready to occupy. You

 a. pack up all your stuff, then call *everyone* you know who has a pickup truck;

 b. call the moving company to have *them* pack up everything and move it; or

 c. pack everything and rent a U-Haul truck.

Moving is much like building a fence except that you substitute construction materials for cardboard boxes and tape. If you're going to do it yourself, you *still* have to buy enough beer to entice people into *wanting* to help. Of course, there are always those people who'll help you move just so they can see what kind of *stuff* you have. They usually make a mental inventory so they can come by later to borrow things.

After eyeballing your stuff and doing a guesstimation of its cubic size, you decide to rent the *big* U-Haul truck. You haven't finished packing (yet), but your schedule suddenly becomes *horribly* complicated by a number of factors—all of which are *far* beyond your control. Work has picked up, so you only have the evenings to move. The majority of your friends are only available on Wednesday night. And (most important) there's only a two-day window for *this* size truck after which you'll have to wait a *month* before another one is available.

You always *swear* you will *never* attempt to move before your stuff is packed because it turns out to be *such* a frustrating pain in the butt whenever you help anyone else (who hasn't packed). You

    a.   call everyone and go fetch the truck;

    b.   call everyone, get them started on packing the remainder of your stuff, and then go fetch the truck; or

    c.   supervise a crew packing the rest of your stuff while someone *else* goes to fetch the truck.

While your friends are busy fondling your belongings and cramming everything into the boxes you've assembled, you have to give a remedial *show-and-tell* briefing to a couple of derelicts someone brought along to "help." Prior to this, you didn't think it was all *that* difficult to assemble a cardboard box.

A *very* attractive woman you know shows up to help, wearing a clingy (and revealing!) tank top and a pair of sprayed-on jeans. Most of your male friends (and some of the females) immediately begin to *drool* on your stuff. You

    a.   get *real* busy, trying to keep everyone focused on the task at hand;

    b.   promise to make introductions later if they'll keep working now; or

    c.   make a mental note to auction off your friend *after* the move is done.

It's interesting to note that many guys become damn near useless when confronted by an enticingly presented pair of ta-tas. I'm told that women have known about this for *centuries*. I guess you learn as you go along, eh?

Another female friend arrives and announces that she's "really good" at packing stuff into trucks. You have no knowledge of this but figure, "What the hell? Why not?" It turns out that she's *not* "really good" at stuffing a truck. She's *phenomenal*. In fact, she has probably saved your move by getting it done in a timely manner!

Naturally, the cosmic energies *must* balance out. Her two teenage daughters are *clueless* about packing boxes, and the three-year-old wants to ask, "What is it?" about *everything*.

It's times like these that'll really put your meager people skills to the test! Good management comes from experience and *desperation*. Have the teenagers pack stuff they *can't* break and that you won't need immediately after the move. A small teddy bear will usually occupy a three-year-old.

Once you've decided on a *do-it-yourself* move and have all the beer, munchies, and pickups assembled in the chosen spot, you should direct the moving activity. A *plan* is called for. You

    a.   tell everyone, "The sooner we git 'er done, the *sooner* we drink beer!" and turn them loose;

    b.   carefully orchestrate the activity, *hoping* to protect your belongings; or

    c.   hand out pre-drawn *pictures* with *detailed* instructions and assign work groups.

Since you're *nowhere* near as drunk as you were when you moved in, you can't remember *how* the hell you got all that furniture up the stairs—past that ninety-degree bend. You

    a.   break out the climbing gear and lower everything off the upstairs balcony;

    b.   *toss* everything off the upstairs balcony while hollering, "Heads up!"; or

    c.   "recreate the moment" of your last move by getting *very* drunk to see if it inspires you.

Since you're living in a "mobile home," you decide to disconnect the plumbing, put the wheels back on, and move the whole trailer in *one* piece (or two). You

   a.   consult the professionals for advice *prior* to having them snag your house with their big truck,
   b.   freak all the way out when they show up to tow your trailer and tell you that you *should* have packed and *moved* all your breakable stuff *before* they arrived, or
   c.   hook it up and *move* it *out!*

When the time comes, you pack everything you own back into the seabag it came out of and examine your options. You

   a.   decide to *ship* your seabag to your destination,
   b.   carry your gear with you, or
   c.   have someone ship the seabag to you after you've discovered *where* you are.

Having loaded all the pickups (including the beer!), everyone sets off for your new place. Somewhere along the way, three of the ten trucks disappear. You have no idea whether they're lost, hijacked, crashed, or broke down. You

   a.   initiate a search for the missing vehicles;
   b.   pat yourself on the head for insisting that all the beer be carried on *your* truck; or
   c.   unload your stuff, crack open a beer, and wait to see if the rest of your stuff shows up.

After two hours, you *still* haven't heard from the missing movers. You

   a.   check the local flea market to see if your stuff is there,
   b.   call the impound yard to see if those "rolling *wrecks*" were grabbed for being a road hazard, or

c. call the tavern to see if your buddies are there and whether they need a *designated mover*.

One of your friends calls to ask if you'll bring your pickup to help them move. Since you don't drink beer (anymore), you're wondering just *how that* is going to work. You

a. show up with a six-pack of sodas and a *huge* bag of chips;
b. figure, "Buzzed people movin' furniture—*that's* entertainment!"; or
c. use the opportunity to practice your Jedi mind tricks.

CHAPTER 23
Travel Troubles

You're driving down the road when the car beside you begins to wander in and out of your lane. Do you

    a.   drop back a bit to analyze the situation;

    b.   speed up to get away from them and watch them in the mirror; or

    c.   drop back, engage the pulse cannons, and blow them off the road?

Once you've ascertained that the person is on the cell phone and taking notes, you

    a.   honk and give them "the *wave*";

    b.   honk, hold up your cardboard sign with driving instructions on it, and smile; or

    c.   fire photon torpedoes to help cleanse the gene pool.

While you're driving in moderately heavy traffic, your cell phone rings (screeches, plays music, buzzes, sings you a stupid song, etc.). You

    a.   ignore it,

b. answer it using your "hands-free" device, or

c. quickly (but *safely*) pull to the side of the road *then* answer it.

So you're talking on your cell phone while driving *without* the hands-free thingie, and someone pulls up beside you, honks, and holds up a cardboard sign which explains *clearly* what you should do with your phone. You

a. pull over and attempt to follow the directions on the sign even though you don't have any lubricants,

b. give the other person "the *wave*" and keep talking, or

c. hang up and call back later.

You're driving down an interstate highway (in a neighboring state where they build roads in a *very* retarded fashion) that is freshly graveled in *both* lanes. Both lanes are *open*, and there are *large* signs every one-fourth mile, saying, "Avoid windshield damage." Do you

a. park your vehicle then wait for the highway crew to come back and finish the job;

b. duct tape your sleeping bag over the windshield then cut a slit in it so you can see; or

c. keep driving, trying to stay way back from the semis that are throwing more projectiles than an aircraft's mini-gun?

So your windshield is *trashed* by the hail of half-inch pebbles. You

a. *make* the truck pull over to get insurance information,

b. pull in front of the truck and shower *his* windshield with rocks for the next 10 miles, or

c. call your insurance agent *while* the pebbles are raining on your window.

You send an e-mail to that state's highway department, asking which *moron* authorized the construction company to repair the road like that since *all other* states do *one* lane at a time to avoid situations where vehicles can't *possibly* "avoid windshield damage." You *demand* to be compensated for your damaged windshield!

Strangely, you never receive an answer from them.

The flaggers on a construction crew are *hard* at work. You actually see one *move*. The rest of them look like cardboard silhouettes. You

    a.   stop to render CPR on the ones who aren't moving,

    b.   toss out a few copies of *National Geographic* as you pass by, or

    c.   stop and share some of the espressos you bought earlier.

Halfway through a construction zone, you're confronted by a bucket loader. This thing is 8 feet tall, 12 feet wide, and coming straight at you. You

    a.   speed up, screaming, "*Bonzi!*";

    b.   take evasive action; or

    c.   close your eyes and *hope* for the best.

You're driving along when someone suddenly makes a right-hand turn from the far left lane across three lanes of traffic. You

    a.   shake your head in amazement, wondering how people like that manage to survive at all;

    b.   wonder how people like that ever find their way home;

    c.   stare in stunned disbelief; or

    d.   notice that they have out-of-state license plates and figure their behavior is understandable since they're probably *lost*.

Two days later, you see someone from your neighborhood abruptly make a left-hand turn from the far right lane without signaling at *all*. You *know* this person ain't lost. You

    a.   call the highway patrol to report a drunk driver,

  b. charge up the pulse cannons and try to blast him as he crosses broadside in front of you, or

  c. quickly accelerate to see how good his insurance company is *after* he hits you broadside.

While driving at 65 mph down a four-lane highway, you notice the person driving the car next to you is *reading* the newspaper as he drives. You

  a. hit your brakes so you're no longer *beside* him then honk your horn,

  b. call the cops to report a *moron*, or

  c. take a picture with your cell phone and send it to that *Believe It* or *Not* show.

At an intersection, your windows start to vibrate from a bass rumble nearby. Someone is sharing their *brain*-damaged version of "music" with everyone around them. The offending vehicle is easy to spot. The *entire* car is vibrating with the beat of the rhythmic *noise*. You

  a. roll up your windows and turn up the stereo to create enough "white noise" to shield you from the auditory assault;

  b. figure that since this idiot was nice enough to share his "music," you'll share too, so you toss a *concussion grenade* through his open window to see if he even *notices*; or

  c. write a *scathing* letter to your assemblyman to lobby for *strict* noise pollution statutes.

At the airport, you run into a *herd* of security guys that are freaking *out* over the stuff in your two pieces of check-in baggage. The X-ray and density checks showed things that looked to *them* like homemade explosive devices (IEDs). You

  a. decide to be as cooperative as possible and let them do whatever they want to do;

   b.   tell them, "That pack is camping gear. Please retie it when you're done. *This* one is my Native ceremonial gear. You may *not* touch these sacred items, but I *will* show them to you"; or

   c.   decide it's not too late to drive.

You're on a plane surrounded by people, wearing *lethal* levels of toxic substances they believe to be "perfume" or "cologne." You quickly find that you're unable to *breathe* the atmosphere. You

   a.   try to hold your breath for the next three hours,

   b.   pull out your bandanna and wrap it around your face—cowboy style, or

   c.   go hide in the restroom for the *entire* flight.

On the return flight, you find yourself surrounded by women. These women are very talkative. Having just finished a *long* business convention (sun dance, summer camp, etc.), you'd rather be left alone, but you don't want to be rude, so you allow them to draw you into a conversation. Almost instantly, you learn that these ladies are all bowlers, bound for Reno's National Bowling Stadium. Once they realize you're *from* Reno, you're immediately appointed "the tour guide" for the remainder of the flight. You share insights about the desert that most people never hear, the rain cycles, the lifestyles of the Native people, and how the area has changed with modern development.

I've always found it odd that people usually talk about the desert being "empty." Huh, maybe they were talking about the *Sahara* or the Gobi Desert, but *this* desert has *lots* of life in it.

I tell people to walk out into the desert, sit down, and start singing. They *won't* feel lonely for very long.

So you've been sitting in the desert, singing for less than fifteen minutes, feeling *very* self-conscious the whole time when you realize a coyote is standing 10 feet away, looking at you. You're pretty sure this critter thinks you're *completely* insane, but it seems to like your singing. You

    a. stop singing and *speak* to the coyote,
    b. break into a medley of songs from the rock opera "Tommy," or
    c. ask the critter if it has any requests.

While riding down the road on your motorcycle, you feel raindrops on your face, but there's not a cloud in the sky. After analyzing the situation for a couple of minutes, you realize there's an English bulldog hanging out of the car ahead of you. This airborne moisture is almost certainly *dog slobber*. You

    a. drop *way* back,
    b. break out your rain gear, or
    c. pass the car then pour a *beer* over your shoulder to see how the dog likes it.

On the same motorcycle, you're behind a truck, and you feel raindrops— that *smell*. When you look, you realize you're behind a *cattle hauler*. You

    a. twist the throttle to pass this nasty thing,
    b. pause for a moment to think about how some people pay *big* bucks for this sort of thing, or
    c. decide it's a *good* time to stop for a while.

You're riding along a mountain road at night, and it's foggy. As you come around a curve, you see oncoming headlights to your *right*. You

    a. swerve to the right, thinking *you're* off course;
    b. stay where you're at, figuring the other vehicle is being piloted by a *drunk*; or
    c. stop to assess this situation.

Immediately after swerving to the right, you realize you've just left the pavement and are now *sliding* on gravel. You're okay until you see a *millpond* ahead of you, and there's *no* way you can turn on that gravel. Now you have to make a *fast* decision! Do you

    a.   lay the bike down so you don't lose it in the pond,

    b.   ride straight into the pond, or

    c.   stand up on the seat with your arms outstretched to go out in *style*?

Having laid the motorcycle down and stopped it—using your *knee* as an anchor—you get the bike up (and shut it off), check on your lady, and assess the scene. You see a pickup truck parked on the *wrong* side of the road with the driver's door open. The driver (a night security guard for the nearby sawmill) has stopped to go pee and is still standing there—*hanging out*. You

    a.   offer to give him some very unprofessional surgery to solve his problem,

    b.   pick up a rock and knock out the truck's headlights, or

    c.   *shoot* out the truck's headlights and ask if the rent-a-cop has a *problem* with that.

You stop at the rest area along the interstate (in another state) and hear a radio broadcast from the US weather service—interspersed with some local news. It's thirty degrees in this bathroom! You

    a.   decide to suggest that you'd *much* rather have had some heat. You could *tell* how cold it was, and you ain't really all that interested in hearing about *wheat*;

    b.   build a fire in the middle of the floor so you don't get frozen to the toilet; or

    c.   decide that you really didn't have to go *that* bad after all. It'll wait.

You're driving through the mountains on a two-lane highway behind a *long* line of slow-moving traffic. When you get a chance to see ahead, you notice that all the traffic is backed up behind a motor home that's puttering along at 35 mph. The posted speed limit is 55. You

a. wrack your brain to remember how far ahead the passing lane is;

b. start to leapfrog past the other vehicles as an opportunity presents itself; or

c. turn off on one of the logging roads for some high-speed four- wheeling, knowing that it rejoins the highway *somewhere* up ahead.

CHAPTER 24
Pets and Adopted Relatives

One of the elders takes care of the feral cats around the sweat lodge and brings the kittens into the house to "tame" them a bit. So everyone can see how *cute* they are. She's always trying to find homes for the kitties. While you're there (on *numerous* occasions), you try *diligently* to ignore them, but since you're softheaded for little kittens, you're less than fully successful.

When two *adorable, all-white* fuzz balls decide to adopt you, you

   a. measure them to see how many carrots and potatoes will fit in the Crock-Pot around them,
   b. "man up" and decide that maybe it's time you accepted some responsibility into your life, or
   c. publicly admit that you're a "cat guy" and *proudly* make a place for them in your home.

The kittens are a little shy about being relocated, but being rez cats, they adapt quickly and begin to make themselves "at home" in two and a half *minutes*.

During the first night, they start *your* "training process" by teaching you how you *should* have decorated your apartment. You were getting tired of those houseplants anyway.

Within the first week, you realize that your adoption program wasn't fully thought out. Even though you *really* scored on one of those scratching pole/kitty nest apartment things at the secondhand store (it was in *excellent* condition!), the little hair balls still prefer to scratch on your hide-a-bed sofa and love seat. Since you can't afford to replace the furniture (you got it in the divorce), you

    a.   go to the fabric store and buy the heaviest material they have to cover the couch and love seat as far up as the cats can reach like a recap on a tire,

    b.   get some of that "repellant" spray stuff that's *guaranteed* to keep all your pets off the furniture, or

    c.   spray them with a diluted solution of Tabasco sauce and water every time you catch them clawing the couch.

Once you figure out that the "repellant" spray only repels *you* (after you've thoroughly ventilated the fumes of it and stopped choking) and remember that rez kitties actually *like* Tabasco sauce, you

    a.   go back to doing the math to figure out how many carrots and potatoes will fit into the Crock-Pot *around* a cat;

    b.   do an interesting looking wainscot-style diamond tuck and roll around your sofa and love seat with the heavy canvas material you found at the fabric store. It's *pink*, but you're man enough to handle it, and it was *on sale*; or

    c.   take them to the vet to have them declawed.

I've heard that being declawed (for a cat) is basically equivalent to us having the ends of our fingers cut off and that some cats *never* recover from the pain. Personally, I ain't got the heart to maim one of my kitties. I think it'd be more humane to *eat* them.

Anybody know how much fourteen yards of Kevlar material costs?

Kittens are beautiful when they're sleeping on the bed with a ray of sunlight surrounding them. It's so cute when they snuggle you and curl up next to you. At 2:00 a.m., a six-pound kitty seems to weigh more like a sixty-five-pound pit bull. They've suddenly gone from being "cute" to *blanket anchor*. When they're a year old (and weigh ten or eleven pounds), it's like trying to sleep under a junk Chevy—that *sheds*.

CHAPTER 25

Holidays

Holidays are particularly significant events, which usually cause their own unique varieties of stresses. There are a number of ways to handle holiday situations—some of which are *infinitely* more successful than others. Some holiday gatherings present conditions which go *far* beyond having to be concerned about your social graces (or the lack thereof) and go straight to having to focus on your own *survival*.

Getting *shot* at a New Year's Eve party pretty much takes the worry out of whether or not you acted like an ass or wore the wrong tie.

It's a matter of priorities.

You're at a Christmas Eve party at your auntie's new double-wide. Your *entire* clan is there, and *everyone* is drinking. You and your wife are having a discussion about whether or not to leave because of your relatives' inappropriate behavior—when your aunt decides to butt in.

Your auntie is (as usual) *very* drunk and happens to be one of the reasons your wife wants to leave. When you *politely* tell your aunt to mind her own business, she suddenly slaps you across the face *really* hard. You

    a.   figure, "*She* started it," and knock her out;

   b.   pick her up by the butt and toss her off her own porch into the mud; or

   c.   leave immediately.

Having opted for tossing your auntie off her porch, you decide that *now* would be a good time to leave *before* the rest of the clan have time to choose sides and retaliate. *Merry Christmas!*

While attending a family gathering for the Fourth of July, you get dragged into the annual "softball" game. This "game" is actually a pretense for a drunken grudge match that's *very* loosely organized around a softball game format.

To be more accurate, it *should* be called "*tackle* softball" since the local orthopedic surgeons always send a free keg of beer as a "thank-you" gift.

When the *first* fight breaks out with one auntie stomping repeatedly on another auntie's ankle, you

   a.   decide it's a *great* time to go pee and get another beer,

   b.   start placing side bets, or

   c.   choose a side and jump into the fray.

A bit later, when a *full-blown* brawl breaks out, you

   a.   call 911 then *leave*;

   b.   kick back to enjoy the show;

   c.   jump in the middle, pull your .357 magnum, and start shooting blanks to get everyone's attention; or

   d.   pull the .357 and use *bird shot* to get everyone's attention.

You and your lovely new wife go to your parents' house for Christmas. A few hours later, your wife tells you that your dad has been pinching her butt every time she walks by and has already offered twice to "show her the woodpile." You

   a.   quietly tell her to walk *way* around your dad,

b. break out your superglue and immobilize your dad's hands by sticking them to *his* butt, or

c. wait until he goes to the bathroom then *screw* the door shut so he can't get out.

While your lady *thinks* she is successfully avoiding your lecherous dad, he sneaks up behind her, holds a camera under her skirt, and takes a photo. The flash is so hot it melts her pantyhose to her leg. You

a. lose your mind and give Dad a camera *suppository*;

b. decide it's the *perfect* time to go *home*; or

c. turn to your mom, and loudly ask, "Hey, Mom! Is his *life insurance* paid up?"

At a family reunion, you and everyone under eight years of age are the *only* sober people in the vicinity. One of your aunties is on a *roll*, stealing power from everyone else by belittling them and invalidating their lives one by one. This activity is *very* hurtful, but state law prohibits anyone from killing her. You

a. ask her how much *she* gets *paid* for being the "liquor taster" at the VFW;

b. do everyone a huge favor and choke her into *unconsciousness*; or

c. *loudly* announce that you consider *her* a *complete* waste of skin, and because you no longer wish to be associated with her in *any* way, you're changing your name to "*Brownlovich*!"

You finally realize (after attending a *third* "family gathering") that your relatives' idea of entertainment is to get *sloppy* drunk and talk bad about whoever isn't present at the moment. When you tell them that sort of behavior is *really* hurtful and *completely* inappropriate, they collectively ostracize you. You

a. apologize in an attempt to get back into their "graces,"

b. accept this action as the blessing it really is and move on with your life, or

c. write a *cool* book about them.

And so it is.

GLOSSARY

Explanation of Terms

ambiance. Fancy French word for the "setting" or atmosphere of a place.

anthropology. The study of people.

appropriate. Politically correct word for "socially acceptable."

archeologist. Person who digs up and studies old stuff.

Bangkok. Capital of Thailand, often called "bang *clap*" due to the causal relationship between R&R and having to get gamma globulin shots afterward.

BDU. Basic disruptive uniform—military issue "camouflage" uniform.

cat house. Brothel.

couth. Old word for "civilized."

CRS. Acronym for "can't remember shit."

culture. How a group of people does the stuff they do.

curare. Used on arrows and dart by South American Indians, causes muscular paralysis.

dogma. A doctrine or belief, a decree, such as instructions on how to pray.

epiphany. An "*Aha!*" moment, where—in some of our cases—we hear a loud popping noise and see a blinding light.

etiquette. The "proper" way to do stuff.

feng shui. The Chinese art of using color and shape (etc.) to bring health, harmony, prosperity, wealth, and other cool things into the home.

flatulence. Big word for "farts."

faux pas (fo' pa). French word for "social blunder."

gamma globulin. An antibody serum used to eliminate infectious diseases.

honky-tonk. Okie word for "bar" or "club."

Hunkapi. A formal adoption ceremony where a person is taken as a relative and given a name.

javelina. Wild pigs which roam in the South from coast to coast.

kung fu. Chinese method for settling disagreements.

meadow muffins. Cattle dung, a.k.a. "cow pies" or "cow patties."

miscreant. An evildoer, villain.

napalm. Jellied gasoline used in warfare.

night ceremony. a.k.a. pipe ceremony or lowampi ceremony, a prayer ceremony performed in the dark.

obscure. Dark, murky, not easily understood or clearly visible.

omnivore. A creature that eats meat *and* vegetables.

ostracize. To banish or exclude from a group.

oxymoron. A figure of speech where seemingly contradictory terms are used (i.e., military intelligence)

Pavlovian. Refers to the Russian scientist Ivan Pavlov and his experiments.

PhD. A doctoral degree—sometimes only useful for serving french fries.

R&R. Military term for "rest and relaxation," sometimes called "rape and ruin" by the less enlightened.

rancheria. What they call a reservation in California.

recon. Short for "reconnaissance" (to look for or search out).

rez. A reservation, also referred to as "the agency."

roof rabbit. This was a popular meat, Felis Catus Domesticus (a.k.a. house cat), sold in butcher shops during the Depression as "roof rabbit."

seabag. Navy term for "duffle bag."

subtle. Not obvious. Usually sails past most of us unnoticed.

sun dance. A *very* involved Native American ceremony, which lasts for nine days (minimum).

sushi. Japanese fish dish served rolled in rice (resembles bait for deep-sea fishing).

SUV. A sport utility vehicle, a.k.a. "land yacht."

sweat lodge. A small (twelve- to sixteen-foot diameter) structure, usually round and dome-shaped (generally made of willow limbs with tarps over them) for Native purification ceremonies.

therapist. Someone who gets paid to listen to your problems and sometimes offers solutions that actually make sense.

tofu. An *alleged* food substance made from soybeans, usually resembles congealed milk.

topo map. Topographical map showing terrain features of an area.

UA. Urine Analysis—a form of drug testing, also tests your ability to pee in a cup.

urban-assault vehicle. More *appropriate* name for an SUV.